Miniature Donkey

Miniature Donkey Owner's Manual

Miniature Donkey care, environment, health, feeding and breeding.

by

Harry Holdstone

Table of Contents

Chapter 1: Introduction

The Miniature Mediterranean Donkey, also known as the Miniature Donkey or the Mini, is not simply a very small donkey; it is a distinct breed in its own right. To qualify as a miniature, a donkey should be 36 inches or 91 centimetres or less in height.

These pint-size equines originate from Sardinia and Sicily. They are almost extinct in both locations, as they have been crossed with standard donkeys in order to produce a more versatile working animal.

However, thanks to their increasing popularity, properly regulated and successful breeding programmes and registries, they are thriving in many countries, especially in the US, UK and in Canada. The US is, at time of writing, the foremost breeding nation of these lovely animals.

Minis were beasts of burden for centuries and were certainly not pets. They were used to carry heavy loads including rock in mines, turn millstones and transport water. Because of their size they could be put to work inside buildings. They are depicted in 18th century pictures harnessed to struts attached to millstones. They would walk round in circles, which turned the stones to grind the flour.

Today some miniature donkeys still work but it is now far less onerous. They may draw small carts or carriages or entertain visitors at fairs, children's parties or other social events. It is now their personalities and other attributes that are more highly valued than their sturdy backs and legs.

Like other equines, minis are herd animals. As a result, they need the company of other donkeys and / or animals… and lots of attention from their owners! Without regular social interaction these lively little animals become very unhappy and even unwell.

Because they are by origin animals from the desert or arid land and also hot regions, a wetter and colder climate is alien to them. However, these tough little equines cope easily with cold and wet conditions as long as they have shelter, food and warm bedding.

As is the case with horses, minis require pasture for both grazing – they are browsers like goats, deer and other animals – and for exercise because they have a great deal of energy.

While they require similar care to a horse (regular de-worming and vaccinations, dental and hoof care) they are surprisingly different in personality. Many owners of minis state they are more dog-like than typically equine as they are loyal, affectionate and form very strong emotional bonds.

In terms of temperament, miniature donkeys are also gregarious, friendly, cuddle-loving, smart, comical, inquisitive animals and they like to have things to do. In the words of Roger Green – the first US importer of minis – in the 1920s:

> *Miniature donkeys possess the affectionate nature of a Newfoundland, the resignation of a cow, the durability of a mule, the courage of a tiger and an intellectual capability only slightly inferior to man's.*

I hope that you find this book both useful and fun to read!

Chapter 2: Miniature Donkey basics

1) History

It is thought that donkeys were first domesticated in Egypt around 3000BC. Whether this included miniatures is not clear, though. The Romans also used donkeys and the likelihood is that this would have included minis from the Mediterranean areas. As the might of the Roman army pushed through vast parts of Africa, Europe and Asia, the donkey would have gone with it.

But how was it that these small, working donkeys left the Italian islands of Sardinia and Sicily and are now found globally as pets and not in their place of origin?

The Miniature Mediterranean Donkey was first imported into the United States of America in May 1929 by a Wall Street stockbroker by the name of Robert Green. He introduced seven minis onto his stud farm in New Jersey. Unfortunately, three were killed by dogs soon after arrival. The surviving jack and jennets formed the foundation of a herd that was more than fifty strong by the mid 1930's.

Grant was followed by other importers, notably Powel Crosley Jr., August Busch Jr., Walter Erman, Richard Sagendorph, Harry T. Morgan and Helen Hayes. Busch's herd gave rise to another important bloodline: "Belleau".

These individuals imported, owned and bred minis because they loved the breed and enjoyed the company of these pint-sized equines. They were not a business venture or a moneymaking scheme as all of these were successful and wealthy individuals. For example, Crosley made cars, Busch was a brewer and Hayes a well-know actress.

While there were still so few minis in the US this handful of breeders worked together to increase the gene pool. There was inevitably some line-breeding and even in-breeding at first. Selective breeding came later when the herds became large enough to support this practice. The late 1930's saw the first sales to the general public.

Bea and Daniel Langfeld, who had a farm in Nebraska called Danby Farm, are widely considered to have made the most significant contribution of all. They saw a photograph of a mini in a magazine and acquired one as a companion for their daughter who had cerebral palsy. This first donkey, Pepi, was purchased from August Busch.

Thereafter the Langfelds bought further donkeys from both Busch and Crosley and so established a foundation herd of their own. Eventually they had approximately sixty jennets and about six jacks which constituted their breeding stock.

In addition to their contribution to breeding and strengthening the gene pool, Mr and Mrs Langfeld also did important work in terms of establishing a registry and promotion. In 1958 they established the first registry for these diminutive equines. This registry became the American Donkey and Mule Society (ADMS) in 1973. During the first thirty years of the registry's existence there were fewer than 10,000 registered animals. In the ten years following 1991 there was a massive increase with US registrations exceeding 60,000.

In 1989 Lynn Gattari of New York launched the National Miniature Donkey Association (NMDA),which publishes two magazines: "Asset" and "Brayer". The first promotes the mini specifically and the latter looks at all breeds of donkeys and mules. In Canada the Canadian Donkey and Mule Association was established to monitor and control breeding and quality.

The next development was shows and auctions. These served to improve breeding lines as breeders had a chance to see minis, increasing their breeding herds and network with other breeders. Shows also introduced minis to the public at large.

Because the American breeding programmes have been so successful, well monitored and controlled, the US mini stock is genetically the most valuable in the world. Many of these donkeys are now exported to Europe and elsewhere from the States and Canada annually. Minis from these bloodlines are between 31 – 34 inches or 79 – 86 centimetres. Common colours are grey, brown, red, black and "spotted".

In the United Kingdom two small herds of these little donkeys were imported in 1980 by Lord and Lady Fisher to their estate in the county of Sussex, England. Their 30-some strong herd gave rise to the strong and successful Marklye bloodline which has played a very important role. There are now several successful breeding programs in the UK. These breeders are also governed by the MMDA.

Thanks to breeders in the US in particular and also in the UK and Canada, there are now miniature donkeys throughout the UK (England, Wales, Scotland and Ireland) and many other countries and on several continents: Australia, Belgium, Brazil, France, Germany, Italy, Mexico, Netherlands, New Zealand, Norway, Spain, Sweden and Switzerland.

2) Terminology

Female minis are called "jennets" or more commonly "jennies" and the males are known as "jacks". A castrated male is, as with horses, called a "gelding". Again as with horses, babies are known as "foals" until they have been weaned. Young that are less than a year old but have been weaned are referred to as "weanlings". Youngsters that are between one and two years old are "yearlings".

3) Personality

These little donkeys are a delight to have around. While they are equines, consensus amongst owners is that they are far more like the family dog than a pet horse in terms of temperament.

When talking to owners and breeders of minis, a set of adjectives keeps recurring: lovable, loyal, intelligent, gregarious, docile, affectionate, cuddle-loving, sweet-natured, eager to please, curious and adaptable. They are also very gentle with children and get on well with most other animals.

On what is as close to a down side as one gets with minis, they need – and will demand – attention and affection. In addition, they like to be busy so they need things to do or play with because they are smart and lively.

Contrary to popular belief, donkeys are not stubborn. This is particularly true of minis. The reason they may resist something is because they are cautious, like to assess things first and have very good memories. If what they are being asked to do was scary or unpleasant last time they won't, understandably, be keen to experience it again.

While horses can be aggressive towards each other (they may bite or kick out) in everyday social interactions, donkey's gestures and behaviours are much milder and calmer. Donkeys may, for instance, lower and shake their heads or give a vocal signal as a warning. Incidents of a donkey injuring another are rare and, when they do occur, they are usually linked to male-to-male rivalry during mating season.

4) Intelligence

Miniature donkeys are smart animals. In fact, many believe them to be more intelligent than horses. These little equines think about things, remember previous experiences and use reason. It is this ability and need to look at and assess situations and to avoid danger that leads to the "stubborn as a donkey" myth. Donkeys simply need time to look, think and decide before acting! Their intelligence and good memories mean that they are easier to train than many other animals.

5) Life span or expectancy

While the average life span of Miniature Donkeys is 25 to 35 years, well cared for minis live longer. Some have been reported to live to almost 50!

This means that a mini is a very long-term commitment and this must be considered when deciding on whether or not to get one.

6) *Miniature Donkey appearance and biology*

Size and weight:

Registries require that the donkey should stand 36 inches (91 centimetres) or less to qualify as a true Miniature Donkey. This is measured from the (unshod) hoof to the top of the withers. However, the average height of minis is 30 – 34 inches (76 – 86 centimetres).

At birth these donkeys weigh 15 – 28 pounds (6.8 – 12.7 kilograms). A mature adult weighs 250 – 450 pounds (113 – 204 kilograms). Just like kittens, very young minis seem to be all ears.

Colours:

Most people think donkeys, regardless of breed and size, are grey. This is far from the truth. The Miniature Donkey is found in an astounding range of colours: black, grey, brown, chestnut, red / sorrel, cream and – although it's very rare – solid white.

Minis may also be spotted or skewbald which are terms that describe white patches on a darker but not a black base coat. Spotted equines have multiple, smaller white patches and skewbald have fewer and larger patches.

Most donkeys have white around their muzzles and eyes. This colouring is known as "light points". Some donkeys don't have this and they are called "no light point" (NLP) individuals.

Markings:

The majority of standard and miniature donkeys have a cross of darker hair that runs along the back from the base of the neck to the end of the tail. There is also a stripe running across the shoulders and over the dorsal or back stripe. It looks like a cross.

Legend has it that the Donkey's Cross, as this mark is called, was placed there by Christ to thank the donkey for carrying him into Jerusalem and to mark the importance of this humble animal.

Other distinguishing features:

There are a number of respects in which this small equine differs from horses:

- ➤ *Ears*: these are very well supplied with blood and much larger than those of horses. This is found in many other creatures from desert and arid areas because ears like these help to cool the body.

- ➤ *Eyes*: like the ears these too are larger than a horse's. They give donkeys a much wider field of vision, which helps them to spot predators.

- ➤ *Tail*: the donkey's tail is far more like that of a cow than a horse as it is covered with short hair with a tuft on the end.

- ➤ *Coat*: the hair on a donkey is both coarser and longer than that of a horse. Despite a longer coat, donkeys lack the undercoat horses have that protect them from wet and cold.

- ➤ *Hooves*: because their hooves are not as sloping, are harder, more elastic and smaller than those of horses, minis don't need to be shod.

- ➤ *Ergots*: unlike horses, minis do not have the vestigial 'toe' in each fetlock.

- ➤ *Vertebral column / spine*: these little donkeys don't have a fifth lumbar vertebra. The only other equine that has the same kind of spine is the Arabian horse.

Body types:

There are two body types found with Miniature Mediterranean Donkeys: drafty and refined.

Drafty: this body type is also known – perhaps more descriptively – as stocky. These minis have wider rumps and thicker legs and neck.

Refined: these donkeys look smaller-boned and thinner than their stocky counterparts.

Chapter 3: The Miniature Donkey as a pet

1) Donkeys, other animals and other donkeys

The chances are that if you acquire or have a donkey there will be other animals in your life too. Given a mini is not a house pet, it will be housed alongside a range of farm animals, other equines and may also share a home with dogs and cats. While donkeys are herd animals and need companionship, it doesn't follow that *all* animals will make good companions. For example, many mini owners say that they are a bad combination with horses. However, they get on well with sheep, smaller standard donkeys and even cows. Two uncastrated male minis will definitely fight.

One also needs to exercise great caution with pet dogs. You need to make proper, controlled introductions as dogs are viewed as predators by minis. There have also been a number of incidents of minis being injured, even killed, by dogs. However, a mini should get used to a pet dog with time and your involvement... as long as the canine doesn't chase or worry at the equine!

2) Miniature Donkeys and children

Minis have wonderful temperaments. The fact that they are very gentle, docile and affectionate makes them ideal pets and companions for children, including very young ones. Owners of these little donkeys report that they appear to especially love children and are particularly careful around them.

Interacting with – feeding, cuddling, leading – a sweet, loving donkey is a wonderful way for children to learn how to interact with, care for and respect animals.

3) Behaviour

Miniature donkeys don't do – or not do – anything without a good reason. While the reason is known by the mini, human beings may find some behaviour inexplicable or even problematic. A donkey always has a motive for its behaviour.

Once you work out the benefit to the mini of what it is or isn't doing you've gone a long way to changing the behaviour. It also helps to have an idea of the underlying cause. It may be one of several or more than one.

Historical and evolutionary reasons for behaviour

The ancestors of modern donkeys lived in arid, inhospitable areas where there were predators, food was scarce and competition for a mate was fierce. To deal with this they developed two survival tactics:

- *A flight response*: a donkey, particularly a mini, has a greater chance of survival if it runs from a predator than if it tries to fight it off. This instinct to run from danger and perceived danger remains. If they can't run for some reason and they feel threatened they will lash out and fight.

- *Territorial behaviour*: the ancestors of today's donkeys were more solitary as they roamed searching for food. When the mating season began, however, males had specific territory which they fought to defend in order to improve their chances of mating with jennets. Donkeys are still more territorial than other equines including horses. As a result, keeping jacks together is unwise.

Because food and water were scarce, donkeys were forced to travel – sometimes great distances – to find them. While this was a hard life in some ways, it kept them lean, fit, strong and mentally active and alert. A pet donkey that is restricted for little movement and is well fed can all too easily become fat, unfit and very, very bored. All of these can lead to so-called problem behaviour.

Genetics and nurture

Just like all living things, minis are affected by genetics; they inherit traits and – perhaps – behavioural characteristics from their parents.

It is also highly likely that young and juvenile donkeys learn behaviour from their mother and other adult donkeys around them.

Environment

There are several aspects of the environment which can have profound effects on the behaviour of your mini:

- The first environmental consideration is linked to the need for mental stimulation. Minis are very smart and curious. If they are too restricted and have nothing to do they get bored, restless and even stressed. All of these reactions can lead to problem and even destructive behaviour. Ensuring that a donkey has social interaction and mental stimulation will help avoid these issues.

- You also affect your mini's behaviour, because you and how you act and behave are an integral part of your pet donkey's environment. If you behave differently it will cause stress, which in turn will affect your mini's behaviour. This needs to be kept in mind by owners when they interact with their pets.

- Changes to accommodations, pastures or in terms of the animals around a donkey will also cause stress. However, making or introducing change slowly will allow your pet to adjust without becoming stressed or agitated.

Pain

Experiencing pain causes behavioural changes in all species. These changes are often quite sudden too. Donkeys can't tell you they are sore but will do all they can to stop the pain they feel. For example, a mini with pain in its back, hips, legs or feet will probably kick out or fight having its foot lifted because it hurts to do so. Similarly, mouth, tooth or jaw pain may result in an increased amount of nibbling, chewing or even biting.

Illnesses or medical conditions

There are normal medical situations, which can cause changes in behaviour in jennets. Females come into heat for four to six days every three weeks except during the winter months. While not all individuals are affected the same way by these hormonal changes, many minis may be moody and move from aggressive to social. Keeping track of a jennet's cycle will help to identify when it is likely to be hormones causing behavioural changes.

There are also a host of illnesses, diseases and deficiencies that result in behaviour changes. These range from life-threatening ones such as brain cancer to food intolerances. Because there could be a number of possibilities, and diagnosis is not easy, marked and ongoing behavioural changes are a reason to get a vet involved!

Learning and experience

Like all animals, minis begin to learn from the time they are born. As with all intelligent animals, they go on learning and they also remember things and experiences. Minis that have not had a chance to learn appropriate behaviour from their mother or another adult donkey may be 'problem' donkeys. In addition, if minis are not socialised by their owner from the time they are young they are more likely to behave in undesirable ways.

All mini behaviour is aimed at making their life more comfortable and happy. So, if your mini rips up sacks and tosses the bits all over the place it's not being naughty. It's simply amusing itself and avoiding boredom.

The human factor

Minis, as previously stated, bond with their owners and are smart and intuitive. As a result of this they pick up on the emotions of the person they are interacting with. For instance, an aggressive or fearful handler will communicate that and the mini is likely to respond aggressively or fearfully.

How to deal with behavioural issues

The bottom line is that if behaviour is uncharacteristic or a problem you need to look for a cause. As stated earlier, minis always have a reason for why they act as they do. Your mini won't suddenly have a personality change!

Once you identify the cause of the behaviour it can be rectified or changed. Some of the steps you should take are:

- Call in a vet to rule out medical problems and pain as causes
- Assess the environment for possible problems or sources of stress
- Honestly assess your own behaviour around your mini in case you are the problem
- Reward your pet's 'good' / desirable behaviour immediately
- Become more aware of your mini's body language so you understand him or her better.

What *not* to do:

- Punish your mini
- Ignore the situation
- Rush the corrective program or training; it will be slow.

Chapter 4: Buying your donkey

Choosing a Miniature Mediterranean Donkey that is right for you is an important matter. In addition to general considerations, you need to be clear about *why* you want a mini.

Do you want a pet and companion only? Or do you want to breed these little creatures? The answer will play a big part in how and why you select one individual over another.

1) How old should a donkey be when you buy it?

Choosing a pet

If you are just looking for a pet, the important factor is weaning. Avoid a foal that is too young to be weaned as they are less likely to be well adjusted adults!

The youngest a mini should be four months old. However, five or six months would be better. Not only does this provide the right amount of time for weaning, the mother also has time to teach and socialise her baby.

Choosing a mini for breeding purposes

The considerations become more complex when you are looking for a mini for breeding purposes. The reason is that you then need to consider both minimum and maximum ages.

In terms of minimum age you could of course buy a weanling and have time to get to know it and bond with it. But, if you want to begin breeding immediately, then you don't want a jennet or a jack that is younger than two, as minis shouldn't be bred younger than this.

A maximum age for jennets is anything up to 15 as she will produce foals safely until she is about 20. Please note, though, that this is *only* true of jennets that have already produced foals. Jennets that are older than four should be avoided if they have never been in foal as it is likely that it will be a battle to get them pregnant.

2) Tips on buying a Miniature Donkey

As with age, why you are buying a mini plays a big role in selecting the individual donkey you want. There are in fact three possibilities: you want a pet, you are looking for a mini you can show or you need a donkey for breeding purposes. What you look for will depend on which of these three applies.

The second factor you must consider when picking out your donkey is that minis live for several decades. You need to select a mini with the short-, medium- and long-term in mind. Not only must the mini be right for you and your purposes, you and what you can provide must meet your jennet or jack's needs.

General guidelines

Regardless of your reason for getting a mini, some things should be done or avoided:

➢ Be clear about why you are buying a donkey

➢ Be 100% sure you can provide what your donkey or donkeys will need for the rest of their lives keeping in mind they will live for anything up to 50 years

➢ If you can, take someone who knows about minis or donkeys with you

➢ Ask questions about the mini's history, behaviour, training etc.

➢ If you want to breed or show minis, you must get the donkey's passport. Without it you can't transport, show or breed with the animal.

➢ Watch the mini as it moves around and is handled as this can tell you a lot about its overall condition and how well socialized it is.

➢ It might be advisable, especially if you are buying a more expensive mini for breeding purposes, to have it examined by a vet. Alternatively, request a written guarantee from the breeder.

➢ Don't buy a mini "sight unseen"; you need to meet it and preferably more than once.

➢ Don't be seduced or blinded by the 'cuteness factor'.

Guidelines for buying a pet or companion

In this situation the factors that you should consider are, for the most part, personal. You could consider any or all of these:

o *Health*: this is a very important factor regardless of why you are buying a mini.
o *Height or size*: this has a lot to do with appeal and 'cuteness' but be cautious of minis smaller than 30 inches or 76 centimetres as they often have health problems.
o *Colour*: this is an entirely personal choice but it can affect price as rarer colours increase the cost.
o *Personality*: you want a mini that is friendly, affectionate and responsive.
o *Price*: you will have a budget or amount in mind (more on prices in a later chapter) so the price needs to fit in with that.
o *Gender*: a jack should be gelded as mating behaviour can be undesirable in a pet. Jennets may be moody when they are in heat.

Guidelines for buying a mini for breeding purposes

Selecting a mini for breed stock purposes is far more complicated. You must consider the following:

o *Health*: health also includes fertility in jacks and whether a jennet has foaled before. A vet will also examine the donkey's "bite" (an over- or under-bite is not permitted by the registries), its stance and back (jennets that have had several foals may become too swaybacked), chest width, jaw shape and being overly "cow-hocked" (when the hind feet point outwards and the hocks point inwards to a far more marked degree than is normal or permissible). You can't buy a donkey that will pass on undesirable or unacceptable genes or traits to its offspring.

o *Personality*: breed stock may not need to be as loving and sweet-natured as a pet. However, it is essential that a jennet is happy to be handled so they can be cared for and you can safely be involved during foaling. A jack must be docile and able to be handled and led.

o *Conformation*: the proportion, size and markings must conform to the guidelines laid down by the associations. These are available online or from many breeders.

o *Height*: if you are considering a jack that is three or more years old then it's better to get one that is no taller than 34 inches or 86 centimetres. Other breeders look for jacks that are only 31 or 32 inches or 79 to 81 centimetres tall. The reason for this is that the offspring may be taller than their sire. A young mini's parents are often a good indicator of the size the foal or weanling will reach.

o *Registration*: this is nice to have and may help prevent inadvertent in-breeding, but it's not essential. If you are satisfied with the mini's health, conformation and so forth you can have the donkey registered at a later stage.

o *Colour*: two factors complicate selecting by colour. Firstly, minis will change colour as they mature and their winter coat is not the same as their summer coat. Breeders consider the summer coat to be the true colour.

3) Is a male or a female better?

Again this depends on whether you want a pet and companion or breed stock.

Pets

As previously stated, a gelding is an excellent choice for a pet as they are docile, sweet and affectionate. Jennets are also lovely animals but they can be moody when on heat. Furthermore if you also have an ungelded jack you may end up with a great deal more work, worries and expenses than you bargained for or wanted when your jennet gets pregnant!

An immature jennet that becomes pregnant may suffer long-term health complications such as bone and muscle problems. She also won't, in all probability, make a good mother due to her own immaturity. Foals born to jennets younger than three are likely to suffer from congenital defects.

If you want to buy more than one mini, acquiring a bonded pair often works well as they already know each other. As a result there is likely to be no or minimal hostility or stress.

Breeding stock

In a breeding stock scenario there are more variables that must be considered.

Breeders agree that it is *not* a good idea to by a jack and jennet pair. It is especially unwise if you buy them as a foal-pair. Before you can begin breeding with minis you need a jack and at least three jennets.

4) One or two or more?

There is no doubt that a solitary miniature donkey is a lonely and unhappy one. These gregarious, fun-loving herd animals *must* have companionship. The best friend for them is without a doubt another mini!

Another miniature will play the same way and speaks the same language. They can eat together and sleep close to each other. It's important and interesting to note that a mini with a loved donkey companion is *no* less adoring towards its people!

A mini that is unhappy and lonely is likely to become destructive and very vocal. They become increasingly needy with their people and may even become pushy and aggressive. A miserable mini will chew and damage objects including quite hard ones like fencing and develop pacing behaviour, which may harm its health.

Goats, ponies, sheep, standard donkeys and mules are not a good idea as companions. A docile, mature horse might work but it's still risky.

Chapter 5: What a Miniature Donkey needs

1) Shelter

It is essential than Miniature Donkeys have shelter so that they are protected from cold, rain and snow, as their coats are not waterproof and therefore offer very inadequate protection. While minis cope with cold they dislike rain and shouldn't become chilled as they may develop pneumonia or bronchitis. Shade from the sun in very hot climates is also needed.

Only a three-sided shelter is usually necessary. The open side must face away from the prevailing winds and the structure must exclude drafts and keep out the rain. In climates such as parts of Canada, where winters may be very severe, a shelter that can be closed may be necessary to keep your mini warm.

Your mini is smart – and has a well-developed sense of self-preservation – and will therefore know when he or she needs to seek shelter and stay in it. This means, though, that there must be access to the shelter directly from the pasture. A mini's shelter therefore should also be left open and only needs to be closed in very cold weather. Some owners do prefer to stable their minis at night for various reasons.

Minis need a much smaller shelter than a standard donkey or a horse. An area of 12 x 12 feet or 3.6 x 3.6 metres will easily accommodate up to three minis in a space that would only hold a single horse, for example.

The floor itself should be concrete. In terms of floor covering, you need to use something that won't be too hard for you to clean (or "muck out") but that does absorb urine. Sawdust, straw – known as bedding – can be used and so can stall mats that can be purchased from equine stores. Don't use sawdust for a jennet about to foal, though.

2) Feeder and water container

Feeder

All donkeys naturally graze at ground level, with their heads down. It's therefore not a good idea to give them a raised feeder of some kind. In fact if they eat with their heads raised they may get food particles in their eyes or ears.

Fortunately this is easily resolved by providing a floor level feeder that contains enough food for grazing and browsing. The food should not be piled higher than the mini's shoulder, though, or particles again pose a risk.

In addition, the feeder must be carefully checked for any rough or sharp edges or areas. If necessary a false bottom must be fitted to the feeder. This is because if a mini presses its throat against the edge of the feeder when eating off the bottom it could damage its throat and trachea / windpipe.

Water container

Like all animals, minis need a constant source of clean drinking water. While many critters aren't fussy about the water they drink, minis are particular. This means that the water container must be cleaned daily.

Self-filling water tanks can be useful as you can be confident that your pet won't run out of water. However, a bucket is also an option as long as it is secured and can't be knocked over and is topped up as and when necessary.

3) Pasture and land

Because minis are originally desert animals they don't need the same kind of lush pasture that farm animals require. In fact minis tend to overgraze, as they love their food so lush pasture is not desirable! This can result in obesity and even serious medical conditions. However, they do need grass to browse and nibble on.

In terms of size or area, the general rule of thumb is that you need one acre of land for each miniature donkey you have. They need grazing and play space but don't run the way horses do.

One way all donkeys groom themselves is by rolling in sand or dust. This is particularly the case in hot or warm weather. Having an area within their pasture where they can have a dust bath is a very good idea.

It's very important to clear the pasture of your mini's droppings.

4) Fencing

Many owners use a combination of plain or woven wire and electric fencing. There is a general feeling that barbed wire should be avoided because of the danger of cuts and puncture wounds.

Electric fencing that reaches about chest height on your mini can be erected inside the wire fencing to protect it and the posts. Minis like to chew on things and rub against them, which can stretch fencing and damage fence posts.

Don't worry about using an electric fence. The shock your mini will receive will not have any lasting effects and, because donkeys are intelligent and have good memories, they won't touch the fence again.

5) Toys and mental stimulation

Minis are thinking creatures. Their intelligence combined with their curiosity and liveliness means that they get bored if they have nothing to do. A bored mini may become a 'naughty' mini.

You can channel all these great characteristics by providing toys for your pet. They don't need to be expensive either as a mini will have hours of fun with a wide range of ordinary objects. Large balls such as beach balls, hula-hoops, sections of hose, small logs, large cardboard boxes (without staples) and even piles of sand or wood shavings make great toys. Not only will your mini have great fun but a playing donkey is a delight to watch… and often very funny too!

Donkeys are known to chew, throw, roll, push, wear or roll on objects and generally get really creative with the things they find in their environments. They play as individuals and in groups.

You can create games too. For example, snacks can be hidden for your mini to look for. Just don't use the wrong snacks / treats or too many of them. The aim is a happy mini, not a fat one.

In addition to toys, a rubbing or scratching post helps a mini to happily wile away some time. A tree stump works well as long as the edges aren't sharp.

6) Other important equipment

There are various items you will need in order to prepare and care for your mini. They include:

- Blanket
- Broom
- Buckets x 2
- Electric fencing
- Fencing stakes
- Fencing wire
- Grooming kit
- Hay / Pitch Fork
- Poop-scoop
- Rake
- Rope halter
- Shovel
- Wheelbarrow.

Chapter 6: Protection – toxic plants, winter care and travelling

1) Toxic plants and your Mini

There are a number of plants and trees found in many countries that are toxic for all equines. There are also those that affect donkeys specifically. It is unfortunately not possible to present a comprehensive list within the scope of this book. However, the plants most often responsible for poisonings are:

- Acacia
- Anemone
- Beech mast
- Black Walnut
- Bluebell bulbs
- Box
- Bracken fern
- Bog Asphodel
- Buttercups
- Columbine (Aquilegia)
- Common Sorrel
- Corn Cockle
- Daffodil bulbs
- Field horsetail
- Fireweed
- Foxglove
- Globe Flower
- Greater Celandine
- Green Potato sprouts
- Hellebores
- Hemlock
- Hemp
- Henbane
- Horse Radish (leaves and flowering shoots)
- Laburnum
- Larkspur

- Laurel
- Lupin
- Mistletoe
- Monkshood (Aconite)
- Nightshade
- Oak (acorns and leaves)
- Oleander
- Privet
- Ragwort
- Red Maple
- Rhododendron
- Snowdrop bulbs
- Spearwort
- Spindle
- St John's Wort
- Thorn apple
- Wild Peas
- Yellow Star Thistle
- Yew (the worst culprit of all).

As a mini owner you're strongly urged to consult a breeder or a vet about plants in your area that pose a risk to your pet.

There are some steps you can take to protect your mini:

- Check new pasture thoroughly for any toxic plants before you allow your minis access to it.

- Monitor pasture boundaries weekly because many of these toxic plants grow very fast.

- Ensure that there are no toxic plants that your mini could reach by stretching its head and neck over a boundary fence.

- It is especially important to supply suitable forage in winter when grazing is scarce to reduce the temptation to try and gain access to areas outside the pasture. Minis are smart and may try to escape…

- Avoid overgrazing of pasture as poor management gives toxic plants the chance to establish themselves where grass would ordinarily keep them out.

- o If you remove or spray poisonous weeds they must be carefully and immediately removed and disposed of.

- o Make sure no unidentifiable vegetation finds its way into hay or other forage.

- o Garden trimmings and refuse may contain pieces of toxic plants so they must be cleared away and disposed of where they can't be reached by your mini or contaminate its food. It's a good idea to mention this to your neighbour too.

- o Fruit trees, oak and beech trees must be fenced off when they are in fruit.

While it may be impossible to remove all plant threats, knowing what to look for and how to deal with poisoning helps.

2) Winter care

Because miniatures don't have an undercoat they need more care in winter than horses do. It's advisable if you live in a very cold area to plan ahead in terms of laying in supplies and making sure your pet mini is in optimal health.

Preparations

Breeders in Canada, for example, suggest taking delivery of bedding and winter forage with extra to spare in case of very heavy snow falls.

It's also wise to ask your vet to check your mini's teeth and make sure that all vaccinations and parasite treatments are up to date and current. Dental condition is important because the drier winter feed places greater demands on teeth and you don't want problems with teeth, eating or health.

Finally, if you can't manage the task yourself, ask a farrier to check and clean your donkey's feet.

Should your mini be kept inside or allowed outside?

In winter you will need to strike a balance between keeping your mini dry and warm and allowing it to wander and play outdoors. A mini that is closed in a stable or barn will not be happy at all. Donkeys cope with cold and will come in when they've had enough and want to get warm. You need to make sure there is always fresh, dry bedding in the shelter.

Weather that is windy and wet is the worst kind for donkeys. A sodden donkey becomes chilled quickly and is then susceptible to respiratory infections. Allowing a mini to graze on frost-covered grass is also not a good idea as this can give rise to health problems.

Blankets and rugs

Miniature donkey's coats naturally thicken as the colder weather approaches. With young and healthy donkeys their coats should be adequate to keep them warm. However, if it is a harsh winter or a very wet one, a blanket or even a waterproof one, may be a good idea. Older minis or ones that are unwell may struggle to maintain their body heat and a blanket for these animals is necessary.

If you use a rug or blanket, it is essential to remove it each day, brush your mini and then replace the rug. Don't use a blanket or rug that is damp, wet or dirty. Having spares is a good idea.

3) *Transporting your donkey*

Transporting or trailering your mini can be very stressful for you and your pet. Fortunately there are steps you can take to guard against some things and this can make the experience much better for all concerned.

The vehicle

Make sure that the vehicle you will be driving and the trailer that your mini will be in are up to the task. On both vehicles check the tyres, tyre pressure, wheel or lug nuts and the spare tyres (yes, preferably more than one). Ensure that you also have the tools you need to change a tyre if you need to.

Paperwork

The paperwork you need to have with you will depend on whether you are crossing borders or, in the US, State lines.

Whether you are doing a local or cross-border trip you will need to have the paperwork for your vehicle required by your local authorities and your driver's license. If you are going to be travelling in a foreign country make sure you know what you need in this line. If you are stopped it will be a dire situation for you and especially your mini.

Your mini may also require papers. Again it is essential to establish the nature of the requirements in the area you are going to. The documentation you need to carry could include proof of vaccinations, a full health certificate or even an equine passport. Don't leave without them!

The trailer

Each breeder and owner will probably have different preferences and theories about the best trailers to use and the best way to create stalls inside the trailer. You will also work out what suits you and your mini best. However, there are some guidelines and suggestions which may be helpful:

➤ If you want to use a divider inside the trailer to separate two animals or for another reason, don't use material with any sharp edges or held together with bits of wire.

➤ Ensure there are no pieces of wire or nails sticking out that your mini could be cut by. If you need to tie anything onto something use twine, not wire.

➤ If you are transporting more than one mini in the trailer don't use a divider that they can't see each other over. Seeing a companion will make the trip more enjoyable and less stressful for them.

➤ The material you put on the floor of the bedding may depend on how long the trip will be. For eight or more hours some breeders suggest a layer of absorbent pellets covered with wood shavings.

Straw is not absorbent and gets slippery when it is wet which makes it a poor choice unless the journey is very brief.

➢ If the journey will be longer than 10 hours your mini will need access to food and water in the trailer. Don't make water containers too full or the bedding will become sodden.

Most breeders recommend you not use grains as they are not properly digested by a mini that can't move around as usual. Hay is perhaps the best feed in a trailer as it can simply be laid loose down the sides of the trailer and your min can graze when it wants to.

➢ Some owners prefer not to tie their minis in the trailer. This allows them to move around and even lie down for a sleep.

If you have an animal that is a problem it will have to be tied. However, ensure that he or she can't get tangled in the rope as this will lead to injuries and great stress and distress.

➢ You can transport docile, healthy minis in a single trailer without using any dividers at all. They will stand together and give each other comfort and companionship.

➢ Opinion is divided about whether or not there should be stops during which minis are offloaded and allowed to stretch their legs.

Some owners believe that it's better to keep going as stopping confuses the minis who wonder what is happening. These individuals also think that it poses safety risks and undermines the donkey's ability to get used to the trailer and relax. Conversely, others believe that you should stop every four hours.

You will have to determine what works best for your minis and for you.

Chapter 7: Training your Miniature Donkey

There are three characteristics that Miniature Mediterranean Donkeys possess that make them fun and rewarding to train: they are curious, intelligent, loving and eager to please!

However, even with these qualities your mini won't learn if you get too pushy or impatient or set unrealistic targets. Donkeys need time to think things through so don't rush the process. If your mini loves you and feels safe, he or she will do all it can to please you.

Keep in mind that your very smart equine is probably training you too. You need to make sure that he or she knows that you are in charge and the 'boss' of the herd. If a donkey bumps you, you need to shove back hard!

As with any animal, the essential elements are not too ask or demand something unrealistic or beyond his or her abilities, to reward good or desired behaviour during training and to finish training sessions with praise, cuddles and treats.

1) Standing tied

This is thought to be one of the most important things to teach a mini because it will be useful in a whole host of situations. If a donkey has learnt how to stand calmly and quietly while tied, you can groom it, examine its hooves and carry out a host of other tasks. In addition, a vet will find it easier to examine the donkey.

Step one

Step one with teaching your mini to stand tied is catching him or her. This can be a challenge but try to catch your mini in an area where it has limited options in terms of movement. For example, catching a donkey in a pasture can by very hard and it may even turn it into a game. It's better to try while your pet is in his stall or shelter.

Don't rush the process and be patient. Don't try and grab your mini either. Even if he or she backs away, let it. If he or she circles around that's okay too. Eventually your pet will decide it would be more interesting to see what you are up to.

Stand close to your mini with him or her to your right and place your right arm over his or her neck. Talk soothingly and provide lots of snuggles and cuddles to keep your mini calm and make the experience enjoyable.

Step two

Once you have your mini, you need to put on a halter. That's step two. A recommended strategy to achieve this is to stand next to your mini's left side, facing in the same direction as your pet. Place your right arm around its neck and hold him or her close while stroking and cuddling your donkey.

Then raise the halter in your left hand until it is under your little equine's chin. Don't bring the halter towards him or her from the side or the front as this might alarm it. Take hold of one side of the halter with your right hand to help guide it on and buckle it. Your movements must be slow and deliberate; don't rush or do anything sudden.

Keep the left side of your body pressed against your mini so he or she perceives that you are doing something *with* him or her, not *to* him or her. If he or she walks forwards or backwards move with him or her and maintain contact. With a very young or skittish mini don't attach a rope to the halter until he or she is used to the halter.

Maintain body-to-body contact, chat to your mini and give cuddles to him or her as you slowly and steadily ease the halter over its nose and then head. The aim is to turn this into an enjoyable experience associated with affection and not a scary and intimidating one.

Step three

Once the halter is on you can attach the rope to it and then tie your mini. Again maintain constant contact, make the experience fun and don't forget to give your donkey lots of cuddles as you attach the rope to the halter.

When your pet is still a little skittish or you think he or she may try to pull away, tie the rope to something that can't be pulled over or out. It must also be something that prevents your mini from getting tangled in the rope if it does move or jump around; a solid fence post or ring in a wall are good options.

To avoid injury or entanglement, tie the rope at the height of your mini's nose. Secondly, the rope should not be long enough to allow him or her to lower its head to knee height. This means the donkey's head is in a comfortable position and he or she can't step over the rope.

It's best if you can begin to train your mini to be tied when it is a weanling. If you buy an older donkey with luck the person you bought it from will have done this training!

Don't be put off if your little equine gets angry and acts up during your first sessions. No animal, especially a smart and active one, likes to be forced to stand still in one spot. If your mini has a tantrum or leaps around, ignore it completely. Don't respond at all unless there is a risk of injury to your pet. As soon as he or she settles and stands quietly you must immediately lavish cuddles and praise on it. You will know the lesson is truly learned when your mini is relaxed when tied.

For the first week, tie your mini a couple of times a day until they are relaxed about it and don't resist being led to where you tie him or her.

Step four

This is an important stage as it is an investment in keeping your mini safe and maintaining that bond of trust. However, you can *only* go to this step when your donkey is truly relaxed about being tied. This level of the training involves teaching your mini to handle having rope tangled around his or her legs. There is a chance that this could happen if a handler or a child is not paying attention.

All you will require is a 6 foot (1.8 metre) long rope. Don't use a rope any longer than that as it could pose a risk. If your mini disentangles itself and bolts, its neck could get injured or even broken.

This time tie the rope at ground level. As the donkey moves around and steps over the rope, its legs will become entangled. Don't leave your mini; watch from nearby in case you need to intervene. Donkeys will struggle against the rope at first. If your mini appears very stressed and scared then step in. If not, leave it for a while.

The vast majority of donkeys will stop struggling quite quickly and will stand still and consider their situation fairly calmly. You will have the pleasure of watching your mini pick up its feet one by one in order to step out of the foils of rope until it has freed itself.

If they can't work it out because they got into a terrible tangle, and they trust you, they'll wait till you get there to help rather than panicking and making it worse.

2) Leading

Training your mini to lead can't happen until it has learnt to stand tied and be relaxed and content about it. One aspect of the lesson learned is that resisting and pulling on the rope is uncomfortable but relaxing and not resisting is comfortable.

Begin with your little equine tied and relaxed. Undo the rope and (attempt to) take your mini for a walk by leading it. Be careful not to step in front of your mini as that might put it off. If he or she won't be led and resists, tie him or her again and try 15 minutes or so later.

If you continue to struggle to get your mini to be led by you, ask someone the donkey knows to help by walking behind it. The presence of someone behind it should encourage your pet to walk. Your assistant can also give the mini little taps on the rump to encourage it if necessary. Walking along a boundary fence or wall can also be helpful as it limits your minis options in terms of which way he or she can move.

As with standing tied, your clever small donkey will work out that it is much more comfortable to walk than pull against the rope. It will also love all the praise and cuddles it gets from you when it walks to lead. Many minis even enjoy going for walks.

3) Loading into a trailer

When you have a mini that is relaxed about standing tied and happy to be led it is so much easier to load him or her into a trailer. However, this doesn't mean it will be plain sailing.

You need to lead your donkey to the edge of the trailer or the ramp up into it. You must maintain even pressure on the lead rope even though he or she will resist. The pressure from the rope and halter won't be comfortable so your mini will begin to inch forward, bit by bit.

Don't rush the process. Don't get impatient and bad tempered. As with all training, try to see the situation from your mini's point of view. It knows what you want but you are asking it to get into an unknown box and it needs to know its okay. Eventually your pet will walk or jump into the trailer. When it does give it loads of praise and snuggles.

If this technique doesn't work and your mini is becoming stressed, there is another approach you can try. Place the trailer inside the pasture area and place some food in the back half. Leave the trailer there with the door open for one to two weeks. Your mini will get used to the trailer in its own time. He or she will jump in and out of it for snacks and just for fun. When it comes time to be led into it by you the trailer will no longer be seen as scary.

4) Final thoughts on training

It is believed that Miniature Donkeys are as smart as intelligent dog breeds. While minis are very bright, some learn faster than others. Also, not all individuals respond to the same rewards or motivations. It's up to you to get to know your mini and what works for and with him or her.

However, some general guidelines that apply to training your mini are:

- A patient, affectionate trainer who communicates well will have better and quicker results.

- Training sessions shouldn't be longer than fifteen minutes and should consist of small steps that are easy for your mini to understand.

- You need to be consistent in terms of communication and rewards.

- Reward desired results or good behaviour immediately.

- Use rewards that are things that donkeys naturally enjoy. For example, food, scratching sessions, social interaction and snuggles. Patting is not a good idea as it may be misconstrued as a smack.

- Don't punish or scold. A frightened donkey will not learn and will no longer trust you. Ignore undesirable behaviour. If you are pushed, however, you must push back.

- Don't beg or plead. You need to show that you are in control and call the shots.

And a final thought: The younger a mini starts training the better BUT as long as it is still in good health, a miniature is *never* too old to learn!

Chapter 8: Caring for your Miniature Donkey

There are a number of things you must do regularly and diligently to keep your mini happy and healthy.

1) Hoof care

Your mini will need to have its hooves cleaned and trimmed every four to eight weeks when it is young and six to eight weeks when mature.

The reason they require trimming is that their hooves are elastic rather than hard like horse hooves. This means that the hoof doesn't wear down. In fact they grow very fast – especially when donkeys are young – and, if left like that, a donkey can become crippled.

In addition to your loving care, your donkey will need the attention of a professional farrier every three months. Ensure that you make use of the services of a farrier who is familiar with donkey hooves and therefore understands that they must be trimmed at a more upright angle than those of a horse.

If conditions have been wet and muddy, you will need to take extra measures. Remove mud and other debris from the hooves with a hoof pick so that bacteria don't breed in the wet areas. If you are concerned about infection, you can also rinse the hoof with an antibacterial solution. Your vet can recommend a suitable one. Follow the directions with care as some cause irritation if they come into contact with the donkey's skin.

2) Brushing

Donkeys really enjoy being scratched and they enjoy being brushed; they probably feel fairly similar. Just remember to brush in the direction that the hair grows and also to be gentle with their ears when holding or brushing them. Use a reasonably stiff brush. You could also use a shedding blade if you need to loosen any thick winter hair in the spring.

A word of caution: Donkeys take a full two months to shed their winter coats. Don't rush the process prematurely or they may get chilled during a late cold snap. In addition, don't groom your mini in winter except on warmer days as it removes the air pockets in the hair that help keep him or her insulated.

You will in all probability not need – or be able – to groom your donkey in summer. Your ministrations will be replaced by dust baths which keep the coat clean and which your mini will love.

However, if you notice that your pet equine is rubbing itself against hard surfaces you should check in case it has lice or fleas and treat it accordingly.

3) Clipping

The Miniature Mediterranean Donkey has not evolved its coat by accident. It helps the mini to regulate its body temperature and offers some protection from the weather (except wet weather) and flies. Lighter coloured and spotted minis are also less likely to get sunburned thanks to their coats.

The bottom line is: *don't* clip their coats fully unless you are preparing them for a show or the vet has instructed that it is necessary for some medical reason. A fully clipped donkey must be given extra protection from cold and wet weather.

4) Mane trimming

You can trim your mini's mane in summer. Trimming fairly close to the neck can look good and does not affect them adversely at all.

Chapter 9: Feeding your pet donkey

1) General

By nature donkeys, including miniatures, are browsers. An important part of grazing is variety. You need to supply this by giving your mini hay, grain and barley or oat straw that he can browse through and enjoy. Straw is thought to help donkeys produce biotin, which is important for hooves and skin.

The only time you will need to supply extra food is if you are experiencing a very cold winter or your mini is either heavily pregnant or lactating. Changes to diet or cessation of food should never be sudden but rather introduced gradually.

Feeds should be chosen with care as minis have healthy appetites and a tendency to get chubby quite quickly.

2) What to feed donkeys

Because these donkeys are so small and prone to obesity (the number one killer of pet donkeys) their diet needs to be carefully managed. Minis require fewer calories even than miniature horses. Ideally your little equine needs to be trickle fed a high fibre and low protein diet as this most closely replicates their diet and feeding patterns in the wild.

Feeds such as grain (know as concentrate feeds) are rarely required by minis unless they are pregnant, nursing or youngsters that are growing very rapidly. Grains must still be rationed and controlled carefully.

The most suitable feed for minis is dust-free grain hay or a good quality grass. It's vital to ensure, in addition to not being dusty, that hay is not mouldy or mildewed. Some moulds have been known to cause birth defects and various health problems in donkeys. Feed should also be free from weeds. You need to be able to trust the source of the dry feed you give to your mini.

During winter your minis will in all probability have reduced or no grazing and be on dry feed only. Come spring, you need to make the change-over gradually. If the change in diet is too abrupt, equines may develop a condition known as grass founder or laminitis. This is caused by grazing on grasses high in sugar.

Begin by putting your mini out to pasture for just 30 minutes and continuing with some dry feed. Gradually increase the length of grazing time each day and reducing the dry feed until, at the end of a week, your mini can be left out in the pasture all day. In the warm months and when there has been adequate rain pasture, grazing should provide all the nutritional requirements of your mini.

It's vital that you monitor your pet's condition year-round and watch for both weight-gain and loss of condition. Changes will mean you need to make appropriate changes to diet. A vigilant owner will also notice if dental problems are making it hard for a donkey to eat dry feed consisting of long fibre items such as hay and straw.

An overweight mini is predisposed to grass founder / laminitis and hyperlipaemia (a severe metabolic disorder caused by abnormally high concentration of fats in the blood). If you need to restrict browsing it's better to reduce the size of the pasture rather than the amount of time spent in it. A further option is to allow a mini to browse longer or more on feeds with moderate nutrition rather than for less time on high nutrition feeds. Minis like to eat!

If pasture feed is sparse or poor quality you could also feed twice a day on some dry feed. There are actually several advantages to this. Firstly, you can control what your mini eats. It also gives you a chance to monitor your donkey's condition and weight. Thirdly, it's a wonderful chance to use feeding time to bond with your pet.

Jennets that are pregnant should be fed a normal diet initially plus appropriate vitamins, minerals and extra protein up until the last 3 months of pregnancy. During the final stage of gestation their nutrient requirements increase. Pregnant and nursing minis need extra hay and a diet with a protein content of 10 – 12%. Grain, high fibre cubes or alfalfa chops can be used to maintain or increase weight with jennets that are not in good condition.

3) How much to feed miniature donkeys

The question of how much to feed a mini is the subject of some debate. If you ask breeders and owners you are likely to encounter the following responses (and others):

- Feed according to body condition. If your mini is getting fat feed it less. If it's underweight feed it more. Make ongoing adjustments as is necessary.

- Feed your mini 2 pounds or 1 kg of feed per 110 pounds or 50 kg of body weight.

- Don't feed more than 2 pounds or 1 kg of feed at a time.

- The average, mature and healthy donkey should have 2 to 3 kilograms or 4.5 to 7 pounds daily.

- If they don't eat all the dry feed you are giving them, you are feeding too much.

Perhaps the first has the most merit as each mini is different and the feed itself varies constantly. For example, each batch of hay will have a slightly different nutritional value. Plants contain different nutrients in different quantities depending on season, location, soil and other factors. It seems to make sense, therefore, that the best guideline is your mini's waistline.

Mini's weight gain in fact shows in several places. Donkeys get crests (fat rolls on the neck) and pads of fat on their sides and rumps. While these may not always be easy to see, you will feel them when giving your pet cuddles. Don't put a chubby mini on a crash diet but feed slightly less each day so the weight comes off gradually. Very fast weight loss can lead to metabolic disorders such as hyperlipaemia. Any change in diet must be introduced slowly.

The bottom line is that you need to monitor your mini's condition and weight and adjust feed accordingly. There are no hard and fast rules or even firm guidelines in terms of quantity as there are with feed types.

This is especially true with minis younger than two and pregnant donkeys. Their condition needs to be very closely watched. Foals should have slow, steady growth and any sudden peaks or dips in condition / weight must be responded to immediately.

4) Water

Your mini must have adequate fluid intake in order to remain healthy. They also need to drink more water in cold weather than in warm weather. This is because their diet consists of dry feed in winter and extra water is necessary to prevent digestive problems such as colic.

All donkeys, including miniatures, are very particular about their water. They won't drink water that is dirty so it is essential to ensure that they have access to clean, fresh water at all times. Water troughs or containers must be kept clean for an additional reason: to prevent the growth of algae and bacteria. This growth is particularly rapid in warmer weather.

There are a number of options available to you in terms of water containers. However, it must not be something that can be knocked over easily or a container that is so low that a young donkey could fall in and drown. Many owners find that a self-filling trough is ideal as they can be confident there will always be clean water available.

Monitoring your mini's water intake in winter is as important as keeping tabs on its food and condition. To encourage your pet donkey to drink during winter you could – at the very least – make sure you break the ice on the surface. Ideally you should add hot water to the trough several times a day; donkeys are far more likely to drink tepid water than cold water.

Adding hot water prevents the water from freezing. Other anti-freeze options are: place a float heater in the trough, cover part of the water surface, float a small ball on the water which promotes water movement and reduces the chances of freezing or locate the water container where it will get some sun.

5) Minerals

Your mini will need to have a mineral lick year round. The contents of these mineral blocks are particularly vital in winter. They contain fortified trace elements such as copper and zinc, which donkeys need in order to be healthy. Your local vet or someone with agricultural knowledge will be able to tell you which minerals are not found in grass etc. in your area and therefore need to be supplied.

Minerals are available in either blocks or granules. The granules are preferable for young minis as they are easier to eat. Usually donkeys will only eat as much as they know they need.

Be very careful to only buy blocks or granules that are for equines because ones formulated for cattle and pigs contain substances such as rumensin and urea, which are toxic to donkeys. Avoid 'treat' blocks too as some contain high levels of molasses which can lead to laminitis.

Mineral blocks can be placed in shelters or in a pasture in good weather so that your mini can use it to supplement its diet whenever they feel the need.

6) Supplemental feeding

The subject of supplemental feeding is another contentious one amongst owners and breeders of miniature donkeys. Essentially it is agreed that some sort of supplemental or additional feeding is needed by:

- Donkeys that are in poor condition / underweight
- Foals, weanlings and yearlings
- Pregnant jennets
- Lactating / nursing jennets.

Healthy, mature miniatures don't need supplemental feeding and it can lead to weight gain and associated health problems. Pregnant jennets especially should not be allowed to become overweight as it could lead to complications with both the pregnancy and the birth.

In fact no supplemental feeding should take place during the final trimester.

If you need to do some supplemental feeding there are several types of feeds that you could use. One option is equine pellets, which are available with a protein content of 10, 12 or 14%. These are often used for lactating jennets, foals and yearlings. The second option is "crimped" oats (*not* whole oats), which contain some fat and about 10% protein. Lastly, you could use what is referred to a balanced or a total supplement. These contain vitamins, minerals and some protein. Never use a product that contains more than 14% protein.

In terms of how much of each to give your mini, it's best to follow the manufacturer's instructions or be guided by a vet. With the crimped oats some breeders suggest about 1 pound or 45 grams per feeding.

Regardless of which option you decide on, it's imperative that you monitor your mini's body condition. You need to assess whether or not your mini's condition is improving and guard against weight gain. Depending on the results you are getting you may have to make changes to feeding quantity or frequency or reduce the percentage of protein. In some cases you may have to stop supplements altogether.

In addition to guarding against weight gain during pregnancy, avoid giving high protein or 'sweet' feeds to jennets that are lactating and during the first week after giving birth. Both feed types – sweet and high protein – promote milk production but that is only helpful if your jennet is *not* producing a good amount of milk.

If she is lactating normally and she also gets milk-promoting feeds she could end up with an overly full udder. This can lead to mastitis (inflammation of the mammary gland), which can in turn result in infection. This is very painful for the jennet, requires antibiotic treatment and makes suckling complicated. To be safe you need to check the jennet's udder to make sure it is not swollen or engorged before giving her any supplemental feeds.

7) Selenium

Selenium is a mineral found in soil and as a result it appears naturally in water and some foods. This mineral is necessary for all equines but is especially crucial for minis.

Selenium deficiencies cause serious health issues including infertility or difficulties conceiving, problems with muscle development, miscarriages in pregnant jennets or foals born with heart and / or respiratory weaknesses or defects.

The mineral will be present in hay and grains that grow in soil containing selenium. Volcanic soil, however, does not contain the mineral. To make matters more complicated, some soil contains levels that are too high!

You need to find out whether the feed you are getting contains the mineral or not and in what sort of concentrations. If the feed doesn't contain any or enough selenium you must provide a supplement. If it is too rich in the mineral you need to source a new feed supplier.

It is clear that minis need a higher level of selenium than horses require. However, the correct or healthy level for miniature donkeys has yet to be determined. That makes it tricky for owners. Minis need selenium but... too much of the mineral is toxic!

One possibility is that when you first get your mini and the vet confirms that he or she is healthy, have a blood test done to measure the selenium level. You can use that as a baseline for that specific individual. A registered and professional breeder and vets that work with equines, including donkeys, will be able to offer advice and guidance.

Obtain information in terms of selenium levels in the soil in your area, levels in the feed you use, how to control selenium intake and how to monitor it. Your aim is of course to ensure your mini stays healthy. A vet will be in a position to discuss options with you and how best to measure and monitor levels in your pet.

You can give your mini selenium in several forms: feed rich in the mineral, injections, mineral and vitamin supplements and selenium salt blocks. While each of these on their own would be enough for horses, they are far from adequate for miniature donkeys. You will need to do a bit of experimenting with combinations of selenium sources.

8) What NOT to feed your mini

There are a number of things that minis should not be fed as they cause weight gain and or health problems. The items *not* to give to your mini include:

- Alfalfa hay
- Clover
- Cereal-based feeds
- Sugary treats or licks
- Straw with retained grain
- Straw or hay that is dusty
- Straw or hay that is mouldy or mildewed
- Unnecessary supplements
- Straw as a hay substitute as it is low in nutrition

If you'd like to spoil your mini with something sweet, place high fibre nuts and chopped carrots and apples with feed.

Titbits from your hand are more a behavioural no-no than anything else. Your mini will remember you gave him or her something and check your hands for treats every time. If your hands are empty you may well get a nip!

Chapter 10: Health management

Miniature donkeys are hardy. However, no matter how robust any living creature is, it is not immune to illness and disease and injuries can happen too. In broad terms, minis need the same preventative medical regime that horses do: regular vaccinations and deworming and check-ups with a farrier and for their teeth.

The second thing to keep in mind is that minis are docile and stoic little creatures by nature. While this may sound like a good thing, it is problematic because it could make it harder for you to spot that your little equine is not well. There are two sure signs, though: the mini isn't eating and / or it is not interested in anything.

If you are concerned about your pet and not sure that it is okay, don't hesitate and rather stay on the side of caution by calling in a vet. Young minis especially can get very sick quite quickly and even something like diarrhoea can get worse rapidly and prove to be fatal.

1) Choosing a vet

You will most certainly need the services of a vet with experience treating equines including donkeys. If he or she knows about miniatures that is even better as they are unique in terms of their needs and some aspects of their biology. A veterinary practice that also provides emergency care is also preferable.

It's important to introduce your new mini to the vet as soon as possible. It gives the vet the opportunity to assess your mini's health and get a sense of what he or she is like when well. You and the vet also have a chance to start building a relationship, which will stand you, the vet and your mini in very good stead.

2) Vaccinations

Many owners and breeders believe minis should receive the same annual vaccinations and boosters as horses in addition to tetanus protection. There are variations from area to area, however, as certain illnesses are found everywhere. Your vet will know which shots your mini will need and how often.

There is a set of vaccines that seems to be fairly commonly used and known as the Four-Way: Eastern / Western encephalomyelitis / Sleeping Sickness, Influenza, Rabies and Rhino pneumonitis (especially for pregnant jennets). Tetanus is also an important, regular injection. Annual vaccinations are administered at the beginning of spring.

A vaccine against West Nile virus is not always given, as some vets don't think donkeys should receive it. Evidence certainly seems to suggest it is not safe for pregnant jennets during the first and the final trimesters.

Vaccinating a jennet a month before foaling is thought to improve her immunity and also trigger the unborn foal's immune system too. Foals are usually given a tetanus shot at birth followed by the first vaccination when they are four months old. The first booster is administered when they are five months old. Thereafter boosters are given annually.

3) Deworming

Miniature Mediterranean Donkeys, like all other equines, need regular deworming in order to control parasites. The frequency of deworming will be determined by the age of your mini and the area it lives in. Your vet will provide a schedule.

If you think your mini might have parasites it's advisable to ask your vet to perform a faecal test. This will not only confirm whether or not there are parasites present but, importantly, what kind they are. If parasites are not dealt with, the host suffers internal tissue damage. While this is seldom fatal in equines it will certainly shorten the donkey's lifespan.

Roundworms are more common in foals and younger minis than in adults. One reason for this is that young donkeys eat their mother's faecal matter. This is a normal behaviour at this age and no cause for alarm; it's the natural way to expose the young mini to bacteria, boost its immune system and so immunize it.

Many breeders and owners are in favour of a rotational schedule in terms of what type of product they use so that the mini doesn't become immune to the deworming preparation. The two primary types of de-wormer used – both are in paste form – are ivermectin and fenbendazole. Both are sold under various trade names. Again, your vet will guide you about which to use and when.

All de-worming preparations are quite safe to use for your mini provided you administer the correct dose. Giving too little has as much effect as giving your donkey no de-worming treatments at all. It can have an even more serious effect: exposing parasites to low-level and nonlethal doses may result in them becoming immune or resistant to that de-wormer. Overdosing can also have undesirable consequences.

In other words, dosing too often, too infrequently, too much or too little will all have negative effects on the medium- and long-term health and well-being of your mini.

Because minis are smart, you will have to find ways to give your pet the de-worming paste. They may spit the paste out if you don't make sure they swallow it. Some owners hide the paste in a treat such as an apple. If you just put the paste in your mini's mouth, make sure you do so as far back as possible and then give him or her something to eat to 'wash' it down.

If you have a small herd of minis the situation changes and becomes a little more complex. It is estimated that only about one in five equines carries a high parasite load. They are also the ones who spread the worms through their faecal matter. These equines are called 'high shedders'. If you can identify the 'shedders' in the herd you may only need to treat them rather than routinely – and unnecessarily – dosing all your minis.

You need to be accurate about identifying these individuals, though, and the only way to do that is through a faecal egg count (FEC). These tests are usually run four times a year so that your vet can build up a profile on each mini. Most FEC tests only look for common parasites. If your vet has concerns he or she may run a full profile test to look for a specific parasite.

If you can use this method to identify 'shedders' you can do so more often and avoid unnecessary dosing of minis that may have no parasites or very low and non-harmful levels. This is better for the healthy minis, is less time-consuming for you and saves money on deworming preparations.

You also need to be sure that your parasite control program is being effective. Two weeks after treating your mini(s) for the first time with a specific preparation, you need to take a dung sample to your vet for a faecal egg count reduction test (FECRT). If the egg count has dropped to zero you know you selected the correct product and administered the right dose. A count above zero means there are still eggs and either you need to discuss another product option with your vet.

A final aspect of parasite control is pasture hygiene:

- Pick up faecal matter regularly. Ideally this should be done daily but the absolute minimum is twice a week.

- Don't have too many animals in the same pasture. Cross-grazing is fine as equines, sheep and cattle don't contaminate each other in terms of internal parasites.

- Don't move recently treated animals to new pasture.

- In the summer, especially if the weather is both hot and dry, you need to harrow the ground.

A final note of caution: as with any medication, keep deworming agents away from children and animals. Equine de-wormers are highly toxic to dogs!

4) Gelding or spaying a Miniature Donkey

Consensus appears to be that female donkeys should be left in tact. There is no reason to have them spayed. While their behaviour may change along with their hormone levels during the monthly oestrus cycle, there are no serious or long-lasting problem behaviours with female minis.

Male donkeys or jacks are a different story. It is generally believed that unless you want to breed minis you must have a jack gelded.

The best age for castration is between 6 and 18 months of age and the closer to the lower end of the scale the better. Some vets also prefer to do castrations during colder weather, as there are no or fewer flies and therefore a lower risk of wound infection.

After the procedure, individual jacks need different amounts of time to settle and behave like geldings rather than intact jacks. For some minis this transition may take as long as a year. While the behaviour of geldings is calmer and more predictable, they may still be sexually active (although infertile) and display territorial aggression when jennets are in season.

Finally, check that your vet knows how to geld a Miniature Donkey because the procedure is a little different than the one used for other equines in order to prevent excessive bleeding.

5) Administering vaccines and shots yourself

Some owners and breeders give their minis injections rather than getting a vet to do so. While learning the basics of how to give an injection may not difficult, you must be shown how to do so by a qualified vet. Not only must you be aware of how to give them but also where.

It's not advisable to give foals injections in the neck; rather give them a shot in their rumps. The area that is usually injected is small and located in an area that is not forgiving about errors: the spinal cord runs above it and the jugular vein below. A lay person should *never* even attempt to give an injection into the vein.

A further safety measure is to keep a syringe of epinephrine handy. A donkey may have a bad allergic reaction to an injection and go into anaphylactic shock as a result. While this very rarely happens with minis, this reaction can be fatal very fast as the airway becomes constricted. Fortunately the epinephrine will reverse this reaction almost instantaneously.

An allergic reaction usually happens within minutes but may be delayed. It's wise not to leave your mini for ten minutes after the shot and check on it for the next hour.

6) Common illnesses and health problems

While one can acquire the knowledge to make a more accurate diagnosis in terms of the health issue your donkey is suffering from, there are some general signs and symptoms all owners should be on the look-out for:

- Lethargy and listlessness
- Loss of interest in activities around him or her
- Loss of, or marked reduction in, appetite
- Inexplicable, marked weight loss or loss of condition
- Diarrhoea
- Growths or lumps
- Weakness or lameness
- Bloating of the abdomen
- Laboured or unusual breathing.

If symptoms persist and / or worsen, or you are in doubt about the nature or severity of the problem, it's far better to be on the side of caution and consult your vet. This is especially the case with young minis or pregnant jennets.

Common diseases and ailments

Keep in mind that minis are laid-back, docile and stoic little equines. They may mask symptoms, pain and distress well so you need to get to know your mini and keep an eye on it.

a) Hoof problems

Hoof and foot problems are the most common health issue experienced by minis and donkeys in general. It needs to be remembered that donkey's feet are not at all like those of other equines such as horses.

Causes

The largest culprit is water and damp. Minis are from arid areas and designed for stony and dry ground. Their hooves actually absorb water so when they are kept in pastures that are damp or wet there is the danger that the hooves will eventually become too soft. Hoof problems can also be the result of injuries or even poor diet.

In severe cases the hoof may even begin to crumble. This in turn leaves minis susceptible to infections, wounds, inflammation and even abscesses.

Common hoof problems and their treatment

➤ Seedy toe: the area under the horny part of the hoof becomes weak and crumbly which allows dirt and even small stones to become stuck in the space.

Treatment involves cutting the affected part of the hoof out and keeping the mini on clean and dry ground until new hoof tissue has grown in.

➤ Thrush: This condition is also caused by damp and wet conditions. Thrush is an infection that attacks the mid-point of the sole of the foot (called the "frog"). One way to diagnose this particular infection is from the distinctive and unpleasant smell it creates.

Treatment may require medication and also involves keeping the mini's feet clean and dry.

➤ Foot abscess: This extremely painful and potentially serious condition is usually caused by a penetrating injury to the foot which then becomes infected. An abscess forms when pus builds up within the foot. The danger lies in the fact that a severe or untreated abscess can result in tetanus, which is a very nasty toxin that attacks the central nervous system resulting in muscle spasms and rigidity.

A vet must be consulted if you suspect an abscess. A less serious abscess may respond to a poultice. A more severe one may need to be cut open and drained. An antibiotic may also be necessary in addition to a tetanus booster if your mini is not up to date with these shots.

➤ Laminitis: Unlike the other foot problems, this is not caused by damp or injury but rather by poor diet, loss of condition during pregnancy or an infection. Regardless of the cause, this is an immensely painful condition that makes walking very difficult. A mini with this condition will not want to walk; don't force it and call a vet. In addition, the effects may have irreversible consequences: the support mechanism for the toe bone in the hoof can be destroyed completely. As a result the toe bone may move downwards or even rotate within the foot.

Treatment will vary depending on the severity of the case. This condition is a medical emergency so a vet must be involved as quickly as possible.

Prevention and management

In very wet or damp conditions it's simply impossible to keep your mini's feet completely dry. However, there are steps you can take to protect your donkey.

Firstly, ensure that the floor and bedding in their shelter is dry and clean. Secondly, clean their feet daily using a hoof pick being careful not to lift the leg too high or twist the knee. Finally, you must engage the regular services of a professional farrier who knows how to clean, trim and treat donkey hooves and feet.

b) Dental problems

Mini's teeth reach as far back as the level of the eye. As a result teeth and gums can only be properly assessed by a qualified professional. Minis and other donkeys are prone to a range of dental problems. This is the second most common health issue with these little equines.

Depending on how old they are and whether it is a jack or a jennet, a healthy miniature has between 16 and 44 teeth. This may include small 'wolf teeth' that have no practical function. Because these teeth evolved to chew dry and / or coarse vegetation, their teeth are long and crowned so they can wear constantly.

As the surface of the tooth wears down with chewing, the reserve long crown pushes through. This crown is found at the point at which the upper and lower sets of teeth meet.

Just like people, young minis have 'milk' teeth which are shed when the adult or permanent teeth are ready to emerge. This process begins when the mini is about 30 months old and the central incisors are the first to be shed and replaced. By age five all the teeth will be permanent ones.

Teeth need to be shed at the right time. If a milk tooth comes out too soon the permanent tooth that replaces it may not be ready. These teeth are more susceptible to cavities and greater and accelerated wear. Conversely, milk teeth that remain in the gum for too long can cause a great deal of pain and even infection.

General symptoms of dental problems

Many dental problems are asymptomatic (have no symptoms) or your brave little equine won't let on that he or she has a problem. When there are symptoms they may include:

- *Problems with nipping* or nibbling grass with the incisors. This may be due to missing, diseased or loose teeth, specifically incisors.

- *Difficulty with chewing* can manifest itself in a number of ways. Balls of food (called "quids") form in the mouth because the mini can't chew its food enough to swallow it. These quids often fall out of the mouth.

  An equine may also take much longer to chew and eat and grind its teeth rather than chewing properly. Finally, your mini may eat with its head tilted as it tries to grind food down and avoid the problem tooth.

- While it may be related to a respiratory problem, minis with dental problems can suffer from *nasal discharge*. This discharge, which may be green, yellow or white, often has a strong smell, which indicates the presence of infection. If the infection is deep or at the root of a tooth there may also be facial swelling. These can be a sign of a dental abscess.

- *Bad breath* is more often than not a sign of periodontal or gum disease. If food collects in and / or around a tooth and stays there it will begin to rot. This sets up inflammation and then infection. The infection penetrates deeper and deeper into the gum and, unless treated, the tooth will eventually be lost. An abscess may also form at some point in the process.

- *Colic* (pain caused by the accumulation of gas in the digestive system) may also occur in minis that are battling with dental problems and battling to eat or not eating.

- *Food packing* refers to the presence of long stem fibres and / or whole grains in the mini's faecal matter. This indicates that the donkey is swallowing food that has not been chewed adequately.

- *Excessive salivation* could be a sign of several problems including gum disease, lacerations, mouth ulcers or some sort of foreign body stuck in the mouth somewhere. It may even indicate a fracture or that the mini is struggling to swallow.

- *Changes in behaviour* are also possible. Pain often causes animals to become aggressive and irritable and may even bite. On the other end of the spectrum, a donkey may become lethargic and withdrawn. In an attempt to ease the pain in their mouths donkeys may also chew on things.

If the situation gets to the stage that your mini can't eat, loses weight and has bad breath, chances are that your pet is suffering from severe or advanced dental or periodontal (gum) issues. These may not be correctable. Don't take chances with dental problems; call in a vet or an Equine Dental Technician (EDT).

Common dental and oral problems experienced by minis

o Sharp points on teeth: these points form as a result of bad chewing movements usually caused by too much processed food. The points, made of tooth enamel, form on the outside of upper teeth and the inside of lower teeth.

These razor sharp points cause pain as they may cut into cheeks and the tongue, especially when eating. This makes the problem worse because the mini will chew badly in an effort to avoid or minimise the pain.

It requires the assistance of an equine dental professional to deal with these points and help to correct the chewing motion. Corrective measures take time and in some cases the damage may be too severe to be rectified.

o Shear mouth: this condition is also sometimes referred to as "hooks and ramps". Shear mouth is an overgrowth in a tooth. This makes the upper tooth look like a hook and the tooth below resembles a ramp. In most cases opposite teeth (one in the top jaw and one in the bottom) are affected.

The causes include poor feeding patterns, the teeth not lining up correctly or a congenital condition affecting the length of either the lower or upper jaw.

This condition results in excessive wear of the teeth affected (the hook and ramp) and poor or restricted jaw movement. In some cases a severe infection or an abscess may develop around the teeth and the ones next to them with the potential for tetanus.

An equine dental professional will identify teeth that have the potential to form hooks and ramps and then reduce the tooth size. A mini with this condition needs regular treatments and check-ups.

o Steps: this condition is diagnosed when a tooth has become overgrown. As a result of the uneven wear on it the tooth looks as though it has steps in it. In addition to uneven and very marked wear, the other causes are the delayed shedding of a milk tooth, asymmetrically shed milk teeth or a missing tooth.

The result of dental steps is not only uneven and excessive wear on the affected tooth but also on all the others as jaw mobility is both poor and abnormal. Teeth and gums may become infected. An overgrown tooth may even penetrate through the mouth into the sinuses, which will set up a secondary infection in the sinuses. The worst case scenario is food particles or pieces that work their way into the bony part of the upper jaw. A case this severe and chronic will lead to the donkey having to be euthanized.

In cases where the step tooth has been picked up early any further problems may be avoided by reducing the size of the overgrown tooth. If the condition has not led to other serious problems, the condition can be managed through regular and very frequent specialist dental care.

o Wave mouth: this dental condition is the result of missing or extra teeth, retained milk teeth, excessive dental wear, gum disease or untreated hooks and ramps or steps. The result is that the cheek teeth arcade looks like a wave due to what has become a number of teeth that are overgrown.

If this condition continues the tooth will be lost prematurely. The mobility of the jaw is also affected which makes eating more difficult.

The reduction of the overgrown teeth (several treatments will probably be necessary) should make the condition more manageable and prevent complications.

o Periodontal / gum disease: these infections are usually bacterial in nature and range from mild to extremely severe. The causes are: tooth overgrowth, injuries to the gum, impacted food between the teeth in gaps called diastema or displaced teeth.

The infected gum pulls away from the tooth leaving a gap in which food particles enter. Food remains stuck between the base of the tooth and the gum. This in turn worsens the infection and drives it deeper into the gum tissue.

Chronic gum disease is very painful and as a result the affected animal will be reluctant to eat. The gums may bleed, abscesses might form and ultimately the tooth will be lost if the tooth root becomes infected.

If the infection is extremely deep the bone of the jaw will also be infected (a condition called osteomyelitis). Chronic and severe gum disease can cause systemic illnesses of various kinds including heart disease.

Gum disease must be caught early in order for treatment to be successful. This is one reason why it is essential to have your minis teeth checked regularly from the time they are just a few weeks old.

o Diastema: slight gaps between teeth are fairly normal, especially as an animal gets older and the tooth roots begin to taper inwards. However, diastema refers to pathological or abnormal and disease-causing spaces between adjacent teeth. In addition to aging, these gaps may be caused by untreated gum disease or overgrown teeth that are forced apart by the pressure of chewing.

Food becomes impacted in these gaps and may enter the space between the gum and the tooth causing an infection. In addition to the dental and gum complications, diastema is linked to poor condition / weight loss and impaction colic.

An equine dentist will reduce overgrowths and remove sharp edges in an effort to prevent food becoming impacted or trapped. In chronic cases a bridging procedure may be performed.

o Over- or under-bite: an overbite occurs when the upper incisors overhang the lower ones. An overbite is when the lower incisors extend beyond the upper ones. Both are a result of a congenital birth defect. In very marked cases the incisors don't meet at all.

An over- or under-bite affects the minis ability to move its jaw normally and to eat, results in excessive wearing of the molars and overgrowth in other teeth.

The condition can be managed by dealing with the results of the over- or under-bite. For example, overgrowths can be reduced. In foals an equine dentist may try to straighten the jaw using orthodontic procedures but this is not always successful.

o Wolf teeth: these two small, shallow teeth are naturally present in all donkeys and are an evolutionary throw-back. Some donkeys may have four rather than two wolf teeth. They don't serve any practical purpose at all and are located at each side of the upper jaw.

The wolf teeth don't often cause a problem at all. If these teeth are becoming a source of pain then they can be removed. Because this procedure must be carried out under anaesthetic or sedation it is best to avoid it if possible.

Prevention

Prevention is certainly far preferable to cure and dental care must form an integral part of standard miniature donkey care.

The first check-up by a professional (a vet qualified to care for equine teeth or an EDT) should be done as soon as possible after a mini is born. This will establish whether or not there are any serious congenital or structural problems. Thereafter, all minis should have their teeth checked twice a year with the exception of old minis, as they may need more frequent attention.

If you pick up a dental problem you need to call in an expert immediately. Don't wait until the situation becomes serious. If you spot symptoms that may be dental-related get help.

c) Endocrine disorders

Endocrine or glandular disorders affect hormone production and that can have serious knock-on effects too. The two that are most relevant with minis are Equine Metabolic Syndrome and Equine Cushing's Disease.

As the owner of a mini you need to be aware of the signs and symptoms of both of these illnesses. Not only are they very serious in their own right, but they are also closely linked to laminitis in equines.

Equine Metabolic Syndrome (EMS)

This condition is similar in several ways to a syndrome that humans suffer from. In humans, however, it is a set of risk factors that predispose an individual to developing heart diseases and / or Type II diabetes.

In equines, EMS is a distinct medical condition. While older equines may develop the illness (in conjunction with Equine Cushing's Disease) it is more common in young animals.

Symptoms

There are two primary symptoms of EMS: insulin resistance and obesity. Equines with EMS are also at greater risk of developing laminitis.

Insulin is a hormone produced in the pancreas that targets the metabolism of sugars, fats, proteins and carbohydrates and makes the transport of glucose in the blood and body. The condition called insulin resistance develops when the body's cells become less sensitive to the effects of insulin. This leads the pancreas to produce even more insulin in an effort to control levels.

The weight gain in equines with EMS is typically found in the neck (the crest), rump and sides. If laminitis develops as a result of the insulin resistance, it may be mild or more severe and recurring.

Diagnosis

The primary means of testing for EMS is through blood tests starting with a base-line insulin test, which measures the resting level.

While horses can be tested after an overnight fasting period, minis must have food as usual. Your vet will probably draw blood in the morning and its best if your mini only has straw for breakfast beforehand.

If this test is inconclusive, a "dynamic blood test" may be done: a small amount of glucose is given to the donkey just before the blood sample is taken.

Treatment and management

The most important aspects of treatment are making sure your mini gets exercise and managing its diet!

Giving your mini toys so it can play and walking your pet every day is crucial. In terms of dietary changes, your vet will provide details about both what and how much to feed a mini with EMS.

Occasionally a vet also prescribes a medication to assist with treatment. The medication is an aid and does not cure or treat the illness and certainly *doesn't* replace the all-important exercise and diet programs.

Equine Cushing's Disease (PPID)

Like EMS, Equine Cushing's Disease is a hormonal disorder. This one, however, involves the pituitary in the brain. Specifically it affects a region of the gland called the 'Pars Intermedia'. This gives rise to the other – and perhaps more correct – name for the condition: 'Pituitary Pars Intermedia Dysfunction' (PPID).

Causes

The underlying issue is damage to the nerves connected to the pituitary gland. The cause of this damage has yet to be established but it worsens with age. As a result of this damage, however, the gland sends out increased quantities of hormone.

Symptoms

PPID has a host of symptoms. Minis with this disorder drink much more than normal and urinate and sweat to excess. They also have longer than usual coats and / or they keep the winter coat for longer than is usual and they are prone to recurrent bouts of very severe laminitis.

In addition, equines suffering from PPID are at much higher risk of frequent infections and parasite infestations. They also develop atypical distribution of both fat and muscle which can make them look pot-bellied and causes them to be lethargic.

Diagnosis

PPID can be diagnosed by a single blood test that measures the levels of adrenocorticotropic hormone (ACTH). This hormone is produced in the pituitary gland in the brain and it regulates the levels of the steroid hormone cortisol. Levels of ACTH that are very high indicate a strong possibility of PPID.

The blood should be drawn when your mini is not battling an infection, laminitis or a marked parasite infestation. However, in order to make a more certain diagnosis the results of the blood test should be considered in conjunction with other typical PPID symptoms.

Your vet may also repeat the blood test in autumn, as ACTH levels are naturally higher at that time of year. Also, a "dynamic" blood test may be required. This involves injecting the equine with something that stimulates the pituitary and then several blood samples are taken over a short period to monitor the changing hormone levels.

Treatment

Given this is a chronic, incurable condition, treatment for PPID is life-long and involves medication and regular blood tests. The medication used by vets is pergolide, which is licensed under various trade names depending on the country you are in.

As with any medication you need to adhere strictly to the dosage and other directions. Sneaking pills into food or treats is often a good idea when dealing with a clever creature like a mini. What can complicate this is that equines may lose their appetites for a few weeks after first starting the medication.

If your mini begins to lose weight / condition to the point that you are concerned, consult your vet who may alter the dose or suspend treatment until the mini is eating again. It usually takes some time and a bit of trial and error to establish the optimal dose for each individual. Furthermore, the dose may have to be changed at various times throughout the mini's life.

While PPID is incurable, with care and the right treatment, the mini's quality of life can be greatly improved and the risk of complications such as laminitis is significantly reduced.

d) Rain scald and mud fever

Rain scald and mud fever are a risk for your miniature donkey if you live in an area that experiences very wet, cold winters and if the mini is not able to access shelter.

Causes

An equine may develop rain scald and / or mud fever as a result of having wet skin and hair for an extended period. Mud fever attacks the limbs and rain scald impacts on the back, shoulders and rump.

Hair and skin that stays wet harbours an organism called Dermatophilus, which causes crusting of the skin and the coat to become matted.

Prevention

Don't groom or brush your mini when it is wet or the moisture will be forced deeper into the hair.

You need to ensure that your mini has access to dry shelter and a hard floor and that there are not a lot of muddy patches in the pasture.

If you are concerned that your mini is not just wet and muddy but might have mud fever or rain scald you should consult your vet.

e) Colic

Although colic is a medical problem with minis and other equines it is not a disease or illness but a symptom of an underlying condition. Colic is the term given to abdominal pain.

Causes

Colic or abdominal pain can be caused by a whole range of problems in the gastric system and abdomen. These include:

- Muscle cramps in the colon or elsewhere in the digestive tract (called spasmodic colic)
- Blockages cause by partially digested food
- Abdominal tumours
- Obstructions caused by foreign objects that have been swallowed
- Stomach ulcers
- Gas
- Twisted gut or bowel (known as "torsion")
- Worm infestation
- Pancreatitis (a serious inflammation of the pancreas).

Each of the above has its own underlying cause or set of causes. With some, such as tumours, the cause may not be known. But there are other causes of some types of colic that the owner does have control over.

Avoid feeding your mini too much grass, a poor or low quality diet, cereals and grains and making sudden changes to your pet donkey's diet.

Signs of colic

A mini with colic is not a happy equine. The two primary signs to watch out for are a loss of appetite and lethargy. As many owners say, a "dull" mini is a reason to worry. Despite the lack of dramatic signs or symptoms a mini with colic is certainly in pain.

There may, however, be more alarming signs: fast breathing; elevated heart rate; rolling; pawing at the ground; decrease or increase in size, consistency and frequency of droppings; excessive sweating and changes in gum colour.

Diagnosis

Owners can often diagnose colic themselves. In order to do so, you need to know your mini well so you are in a position to pick up changes in behaviour, breathing, sweating etc. quickly. You also must be familiar with your pet's eating patterns and the average quantity and usual consistency of its droppings. This can be done when cleaning out the pasture.

While you may have a pretty good idea that your mini is suffering from colic, you need a vet to diagnose the underlying condition. Some are very serious and need to be treated as soon as possible.

The standard steps your vet will take are to take your mini's temperature, listen to its heart rate, take blood samples to run tests, listen to the abdomen for the presence or absence of normal bowel and gut sounds and perform a rectal examination. Your vet will also ask you a number of questions about diet, eating patterns and various other aspects of your mini's behaviour.

Treatment

It's not a good idea to treat colic yourself because the potential causes are so numerous. The course of treatment your mini is given will depend on the underlying condition your vet has diagnosed.

These may range from pain killers and antibiotics right through to hospitalisation and surgery. If the diagnosis is serious indeed and the prognosis is very poor, your vet may recommend euthanasia. If your mini must be hospitalised, its companion animal must go with it to reduce stress as it can lead to complications or other conditions.

Prevention

Some underlying reasons for your mini developing colic, such as tumours, can't be avoided no matter how well you care for your pet. But there are some things you can do:

- ✓ Know your Miniature Donkey in terms of its behaviour
- ✓ Monitor its droppings for frequency and consistency
- ✓ Follow good feeding practices: good quality food, introduce changes gradually, don't use grains and high protein feeds and follow a regular feeding schedule
- ✓ Ensure there is always a supply of clean fresh water
- ✓ Don't allow too much grass grazing, especially in early spring and on sandy ground
- ✓ Keep the pasture and shelter free of foreign objects such as plastic, rope etc. that could be swallowed
- ✓ Fence of fruit trees so your mini can't overindulge
- ✓ Administer an appropriate and effective deworming program
- ✓ Have your mini's teeth checked and cared for regularly

All of these will reduce the chance of your mini developing some of the conditions that give rise to painful and distressing bouts of colic.

f) Hyperlipaemia

Hyperlipaemia means too much fat in the blood. This is a potentially fatal condition and has a poor prognosis even when treated quickly.

Miniature Mediterranean Donkeys are particularly at risk because their constitutions evolved to feed on sparse, scrubby plants and grasses and to walk great distances each day to find food. If this kind of body and metabolism is then placed in lush pastures where it gets limited exercise, you have a high risk situation in terms of developing hyperlipaemia.

The bizarre aspect of this condition is that it doesn't develop until the mini – which may well be carrying extra weight – stops eating for some reason.

Progress of the disease

A mini, that suddenly stops eating, for whatever reason, begins to use more energy than it takes in. In order to fuel itself, the body starts to use the energy that is stored as fat deposits. Free fatty acids are circulated to the liver where they are converted into glucose, which will be used for energy.

Normally a number of glands and the hormones they produce control and regulate the release of the fat cells from fat stores and stop the process if the liver can't cope or the body has enough glucose. Minis don't have the ability to regulate or properly stop the release and flow of these fats in the blood.

As a result the blood begins to become increasingly full of fat cells, which circulate throughout the body. This large amount of fat in the blood causes degeneration and failure of internal organs, beginning with the liver and kidneys. Organ failure is irreversible and results in death.

Risk factors

Certain types or groups of minis are at higher risk of developing hyperlipaemia.

Jennets are more likely to develop this condition than jacks, especially if they are pregnant or lactating. Any mini that is overweight is more at risk but thin or underweight minis have been known to become ill especially if the weight loss has been sudden.

Stress can also cause a loss of appetite, which can trigger hyperlipaemia. Sources of stress for a mini include travel, pain, the loss of a companion, a sudden change in diet or routine or the introduction of new animals.

Medical conditions such as dental problems, colic, parasites etc. that cause a loss of appetite also predispose minis to this very serious illness.

Symptoms

The initial signs of hyperlipaemia are behavioural and usually small or subtle. An owner that knows their mini really well will pick them up. An owner who hasn't taken the time to become familiar with their pet equine won't… and the consequences could be fatal.

If your mini has stopped eating, is lethargic, is producing fewer droppings or they are mucous-covered, has bad breath and seems under the weather *don't* delay: call your vet! Any delay with treating hyperlipaemia reduces the chances of preventing organ damage and worse.

A mini that is pressing its head against objects, circling, has fluid build-up in its tissue or is experiencing involuntary muscle movements (ataxia) is already suffering from kidney and / or liver failure. Collapse and seizures are usually followed by death.

Treatment

The vet will perform a blood test. A visual examination of the blood sample under a microscope shows that, once the red blood cells have settled, there are fat molecules floating in the serum. Vets can accurately measure the fat levels by looking at the triglyceride count.

The most important course of action for treating a miniature donkey with hyperlipaemia in order to prevent organ damage is to get it to eat. If the mini has no appetite and refuses food the vet may feed it via a gastric tube, which goes through the nose and into the stomach. A donkey that is already very weak may also need to be placed on a drip to help to rehydrate it.

If hospitalisation is required, your mini's companion animal must go with it to reduce stress.

Prevention

While you can't guard and protect your mini completely against this terrible illness there are precautions you can take and things you can do which reduce the risks:

- Don't let your mini become over- or under-weight
- Minimise stress: introduce all changes slowly whether they are changes in diet or environment, the introduction of a new animal or transporting your mini
- Keep your little donkey warm in cold weather and make sure it can come out of the cold and wind
- Ensure minis stay dry or at least don't become chilled in wet weather.

g) Respiratory illnesses

The respiratory system is larger than many realise. It begins with the nose and includes the windpipe or trachea and the lungs and all their structures. Debris trapped in the nose and or the mucous in the system is sneezed or coughed out in normal circumstances.

Although donkeys, including minis, and horses suffer from the same respiratory diseases, minis are stoic about it; horses kick up a fuss and let you know they are sick. The danger is that your mini might be very sick before you spot the problem.

Causes

There are several possible causes or underlying issues that give rise to respiratory problems in minis.

The first and perhaps most common cause is infection that can be either bacterial or viral in nature. In terms of viral infections, donkeys may contract Equine Influenza, Equine Herpes or the donkey-specific form of herpes called Asinine Herpes Virus. A common bacterial infection is called Strangles, which is caused by *Streptococcus equi*. Minis that have become chilled may also suffer from infections that lead to bronchitis or even pneumonia.

Like people, donkeys battle with allergies and may develop a condition similar to asthma. A mini might react to spores, pollen or dust. In chronic or severe cases this may result in a condition called Recurrent Airway Obstruction.

Fortunately they are rare, but some minis may develop tumours in the lungs.

There is also a nasty parasite that infests the lungs and causes great respiratory distress: the equine lungworm.

As a consequence of a serious respiratory condition, a mini may suffer from complications. One is fibrosis, which refers to a loss of elasticity in the lung tissue which makes breathing difficult. Fibrosis can occur as a function of aging too. The second potential complication is the narrowing or even the collapse of the trachea, which can then no longer function properly.

Symptoms

The average rate of respiration (how often an animal breathes in and out) for a mini is 20 times a minute. However, you need to become familiar with your mini's respiration rate, as some are as low as 12 and others breathe as rapidly as 30 times a minute. A marked change in respiration rate should raise a red flag for you.

Other common symptoms of respiratory disease include:

- A persistent cough
- Noisy or harsh-sounding respiration
- Flaring nostrils as a breath is taken
- Excessive or very marked chest or abdominal movement
- An outstretched neck
- Swollen lymph nodes below the lower jaw and in the neck
- Nasal discharge from one or both nostrils
- Loss of appetite
- Lethargy
- Fever.

Diagnosis

If you suspect that your mini has a respiratory condition of some sort you need to call your vet immediately.

The vet will listen to your mini's lungs for heart and respiration rates and take its temperature. A general examination will also be done and samples of discharge, blood and even droppings may be taken for analysis.

You will be asked by the vet about your pet's eating patterns, breathing, de-worming and vaccination history to establish that they are up to date, any changes such as different bedding material and recent travel and contact with other equines. Provide any and all information that may be relevant and helpful in making an accurate diagnosis.

Treatment

The form that the treatment takes will depend on the cause of the respiratory problem. For example, bacterial infections will be treated with antibiotics, several conditions will benefit from the use of anti-inflammatories and bronchodilators that open up the airways and reduce mucous production.

If your vet is concerned about a tumour or some other deep tissue problem, a lung biopsy may be performed.

Allergy-based breathing problems will require changes and management. For instance, you may need to make changes to bedding and make your mini's environment dust free.

Prevention

You can't protect your mini completely but there are things you can do to reduce the risk of respiratory conditions in your little equine.

A vaccination in the form of an annual booster will help guard against Equine Influenza. An effective deworming program is also helpful as is ensuring that both bedding and feed are as dust-free as possible.

Keeping your pet's shelter clean and dry is also important. Clean out any damp or dirty bedding before it has a chance to become mouldy or mildewed. Keep the stall dry and clean and disinfect it regularly.

h) Sarcoids (skin tumours)

Sarcoids are fairly common cancerous tumours that grow on the skin. They are found on the legs, heads and bodies. These tumours can appear very suddenly and – more alarmingly – some types often grow very rapidly. The good news is they remain in skin tissue and do not move deeper or affect internal organs.

Symptoms

Different kinds of sarcoids look different. There are six types: fibroblastic, malevolent, mixed, nodular, occult and verrucose.

Verrucose sarcoids resemble warts as they are grey and can look scabby with little lumps within them. As the name indicates, the malevolent sarcoids are the most aggressive and spread rapidly and across large areas. They are a rarer type and when they do occur they are usually found on the elbows or face.

Other sarcoids are quite fleshy and resemble large moles. This type is prone to develop where the skin was previously injured. Yet others form lumps of various sizes, which may ulcerate and bleed or release a clear fluid. Other tumours are flat, circular in shape and no hair grows on that spot.

Causes

Some donkeys seem to have a genetic predisposition to developing these skin growths. Evidence has come to light that sarcoids are caused by a particle that has virus-like qualities that is transmitted by flies. In addition, this makes sarcoids infectious.

Treatment

The earlier sarcoids are treated the better. Given most owners won't be able to establish which type of sarcoid their mini has it's not wise to try and treat these growths yourself.

Treatment will vary depending on which type your donkey has. It may involve something as easy as the application of a cream or ointment, tying off the growth to starve it of blood (a technique called ligation), freezing the tumour off using liquid nitrogen (known as cryosurgery), and injections to kill the cancer cells, surgery, and chemotherapy or radiation therapy.

It should be acknowledged that treating these growths takes time, money and a successful outcome is not always achievable. About 50% of sarcoids will grow again.

Management

You can't prevent sarcoids but you can reduce the risk slightly and improve the prognosis if your mini develops a growth.

As with any medical condition it is really important to spot these tumours early. As you give your mini its daily feed and cuddle, check it for any lumps. Using a fly deterrent will also help to prevent the virus linked to sarcoids from spreading to other parts of the body and other equines.

i) Atypical myopathy

Atypical myopathy (AM) is a metabolic disease that affects the muscles and is life-threatening with a mortality rate of about 70%. Although horses are more often affected, there have been some cases of donkeys becoming ill with AM.

Death can occur anywhere from 12 hours to 10 days after the first signs and symptoms develop.

Causes

This serious illness is relatively new and as a result it is not yet entirely understood. However, evidence thus far seems to indicate that the cause is a plant toxin. In the UK and Europe the culprit is the seeds and leaves of the Sycamore tree (*Acer pseudoplatanus*) and in the US the seeds of the Box Elder (*Acer negundo*) are thought to be responsible. These trees contain a toxin called hypoglycin A and it is this that is believed to lead to AM.

Symptoms

The symptoms of this type of poisoning and AM are dramatic: loss of appetite, excessive sweating, dark red urine, choke (inability to swallow), very marked lethargy, increased respiration and heart rates, muscle weakness, dark red gums and an inability to stand.

Prevention and management

The time to be extremely vigilant and take extra precautions is autumn when the seeds are ripe and winds or water carry them away from the trees. This means that seeds can blow or wash onto your pasture even if the tree is some distance away. Even more alarmingly, in very wet weather the toxins can leach out of the seeds into the spoil.

Make sure you can identify sycamore or box elders, their seeds and leaves. If there are any trees on your land you need to at least fence them off so your mini can't eat the leaves or seeds. Look for and remove leaves and seeds from the pasture daily; this can be combined with collecting droppings.

Your mini is also far less likely to eat things it shouldn't if you ensure that he or she has enough to eat.

Monitor your mini for signs and symptoms daily during the period that the sycamores and box elders are producing seeds. If you notice anything untoward, contact your vet immediately.

j) Plant poisoning

Just as there are a large number of plants that are toxic for your mini if ingested, the symptoms of plant poisoning also vary greatly.

They include: excessive sweating, jaundice, lethargy, irritability, excitability, weight loss, convulsions, poor co-ordination, frothing at the mouth, excessive salivation, dilated pupils, regurgitation, diarrhoea, blindness, haemorrhage, muscle tremors or twitches, photosensitivity, staggering, inability to stand, blisters in the mouth, jaw clamping, dark or bloody urine, breathing difficulty, an increased or decreased heart rate, paralysis and kidney failure.

If you notice any or a combination of these don't try to deal with it yourself. Call a vet immediately.

k) West Nile Virus

West Nile Virus, as the name implies, is found in Africa. However, it is not only North Africa but the whole continent down to southern Africa. It has also been identified in Asia (west and central), the Middle East, the Mediterranean region, Eastern Europe, the Rhone delta in France and in New York State, the East Coast, Midwest and southern states of America. The strains found in the US are thought to originate in the Middle East.

Causes

The arbovirus (genus *Flavivirus* and family *Flaviviridae*) is carried by birds and then transmitted by mosquitoes.

Migrating birds may be one reason why the virus has spread to several continents. Unlike with malaria, this nasty organism is transmitted by no fewer than 29 species of mosquito in North America alone. Infected equines don't infect each other.

Once an equine has been bitten by an infected mosquito the incubation period for the virus is 5 to 15 days. Some animals that get sick develop very serious neurological symptoms and conditions. Minis and young horses are more likely to develop symptoms and become ill. There have been cases of horses and standard donkeys that didn't develop symptoms at all. Mortality rates range between 25 and 45%.

Symptoms

This virus causes neurologic disease. Because the central nervous system and brain are affected, West Nile Virus leads to a range of alarming symptoms.

Affected equines will stop eating, experience muscle spasms and / or twitches, develop encephalitis (an inflammation of the brain), have trouble seeing and / or swallowing, circle or move aimlessly, grind their teeth, become partially paralysed and / or have convulsions. The virus can also cause sleepiness, extreme lethargy, weakness, anxiety, fever, total paralysis and hyper-excitability. Coma usually precedes death.

Some symptoms and damage such as brain lesions are only found if a post-mortem is performed.

Diagnosis

Diagnosis is not easy because the symptoms are not unique to West Nile Virus. The only way to make a definitive diagnosis is through targeted laboratory tests. In other words, these tests look specifically for antigens of this virus. These are performed on blood samples or fluid taken from the spinal cord.

Treatment

There is no treatment for viruses and this one is no exception. It must be allowed to run its course and all the care given to an infected equine is supportive and aimed at easing symptoms.

l) Flies and midges

Flies and midges can cause some health problems and at best they will annoy, irritate and distress your miniature.

Flies

There are several types of flies that may be drawn to equines including donkeys. As the owner of a mini you need to watch for signs that your pet is being bothered by flies.

Your pint sized donkey will stamp its feet, swish its tail and toss and shake its head in order to chase away flies circling or sitting on it. The bites from more aggressive, larger flies such as horseflies could leave raised bumps, some of which may even bleed slightly.

While flies will be an unavoidable part of your mini's life, you can help to deter them and at least reduce the numbers:

- Remove dung from pastures
- Keeping shelters clean
- Remove uneaten food
- Keep feed and water troughs hygienic
- Use fly traps or strips
- Apply cream or spray repellents twice daily

When using repellents, test some of it on a small patch to make sure that your mini doesn't have an allergic reaction to the product. While some owners use herbal or plant-based repellents, there is not a great deal of scientific evidence to prove that they do work.

Midges

There are hundreds of different species of midge worldwide and they all cause various animals a great deal of distress, discomfort and annoyance. In the UK the worst culprit is the *Culicoides* midge. Its bite, in equines that are allergic to the midge's saliva, causes a nasty skin condition known as "Sweet Itch".

Some reactions to midge bites, including "Sweet Itch", are so severe that the mini will rub itself almost constantly against things in order to try and ease the itch. They can do so much scratching and rubbing that they become raw and may even make their skin bleed. This in turn attracts more midges (and flies).

In some regions, preventative measures need to be adopted in spring, summer and autumn, especially at dawn and dusk. Other areas may not suffer from such a prolonged midge season.

In terms of what can be done to keep midges at bay, there are both chemical and other methods available to you. Wet ground and soil, which is mainly clay-based, will be more midge-filled so keeping your mini away from sites like these will help. Keep the stable free of damp bedding and excess or old food.

You could also buy your mini a fly sheet or rug to provide protection. A further option is overlapping plastic strips on windows and doors. Make sure, however, that you introduce them gradually so as not to stress or frighten your mini.

Fly repellents often work well on midges too. You need to exercise great caution, though, as most of them can't be used on broken skin and others may cause an allergic reaction. Be guided by your vet in the choice of a preparation and follow the vet or the manufacturer's directions.

m) Ticks

Ticks, like fleas, are parasites that feed on the host's blood. There are some tick species that are found all over the world and others that are specific to certain continents and locations.

Ticks are more prevalent in some areas such as those where there is long grass or other untreated livestock. These insects are also more of a problem in spring and summer than during colder times of the year.

It can be fairly easy to spot ticks. You will also feel them when you cuddle, pet or groom your pet. Ticks engorged with blood are especially hard to miss as they become large and bloated.

Different tick species are different sizes and colours. They are often found on parts of a donkey where the blood supply is close to the surface and the tick is protected and harder to rub off such as the ears, under the tail and between the back legs.

Treatment and prevention

Removing a tick that has gorged itself on your mini's blood is not a pleasant experience for either of you. It's also not easy to remove some ticks. If they are not removed at all or completely they don't just cause irritation to your pet; they may also pose dangers to your donkey as they may carry serious diseases.

Some vets and equine stockists of equine supplies sell tick removers: devices that are ideal for removing ticks from your mini. Older methods such as smothering the tick in something oily or greasy (like Vaseline) or burning them should *not* be used as they usually cause the dying tick to regurgitate which forces toxins into the host's bloodstream.

Ideally you want to keep ticks away or prevent them rather than dealing with them once they have latched onto your pet. However, options are limited.

Some owners have had success using anti-tick shampoo designed for dogs. These kill ticks on contact. You must check with an equine vet first before using any product to make sure it is safe for your mini and will do the job. Your vet or local donkey sanctuary may be able to suggest better or other options.

Removing ticks from your pet donkey and keeping them away is one part of the war against these nasty parasites. You also need to treat the environment in which your mini lives. You could perhaps use one of the granular, spray or powdered products that are sprinkled or sprayed on the ground, bedding and other areas your pet uses. These are available from pet stores, online and vets. It is crucial, though, to ensure you use a product that will not be harmful or toxic if ingested or on contact.

There are a large number of different ticks. Some tick bites will also cause local irritation. Others are potentially far more serious. While some carry the same diseases, others are specific to one species of tick. What's more, certain tick species carry more than one disease. Tick-borne diseases can be hard to spot. There are several common diseases that affect both minis and, often, humans:

▪ Lyme disease: This infection attacks both equines and people and leads to lameness. In worst case scenarios or severe cases this illness is fatal. Diagnosis is difficult as many of the symptoms mimic other illnesses.

Symptoms may be slow to emerge and can come and go. The primary symptoms are short-term lameness that lasts several days, fatigue and lethargy and loss of appetite.

- Tick paralysis: This is not so much a disease as a very severe reaction to the toxin that ticks secrete. This toxin attacks the central nervous system.

  Symptoms include loss of appetite, nausea, inability to regulate body temperature, weakness, lethargy and partial or full paralysis. More severe symptoms are difficulty swallowing and then with breathing. Death usually follows.

When minis stop eating they are at risk of also developing hyperlipaemia in addition to the tick paralysis.

n) Lice and mites

Lice

Lice are another group of parasitic insects. They are much smaller than ticks and are found all over the world, regardless of climate. Some lice suck the host's blood as ticks do and others are called chewing or biting lice. The latter type of louse feed on skin secretions and hair and skin debris. They lack the piercing mouthparts that the blood-sucking lice have.

Unlike many insects that are more prevalent in the warmer months, lice infestations are an issue in late winter and early spring. There will be a natural decline in lice numbers in summer when the equine's hair is dryer and the insects are exposed to sun and moving air. A few lice remain dormant on some animals and, come winter, they will multiply, re-infest the host and any other animals nearby.

Lice don't actually pose much of a health risk to your mini at all unless the infestation is severe or the donkey is very young or very old. However, the bites cause itching and irritation which is unpleasant for your little equine. If the itching becomes severe your mini may rub itself raw which makes the skin vulnerable to flies and bacteria.

You will know your mini has lice because, despite how small they are, you will be able to spot them when you are close. You will also notice the behaviour described above that indicates chronic itching. Lice don't create scabs or sores, though.

In terms of prevention, there are several practical steps one can take. Equines that are well fed and kept dry in winter will be in better condition and have strong immune systems. This will make them more resistant and less likely to become badly infested. In addition, don't overcrowd animals as they cross-infest each other. Thirdly, if one mini in the herd has a bad case of lice you need to treat all of your little donkeys.

There are chemical agents available to deal with lice you can buy from pet stores, online and from your vet. However, not all of them are safe for equines including donkeys. You also need to be confident that you use a product that will not be harmful or toxic if ingested or on contact.

Some of these products are effective on sucking lice but not chewing lice. It must also be a preparation that deals with lice at each stage of their life cycle including the eggs, which are called nits. You also need to clean out and treat your mini's shelter or stall and ensure you change the bedding regularly.

Mites

Mites are even smaller than lice and most species live on the skin. There are four species of mites globally that are a problem for equines. Only two of them affect donkeys, including miniatures: *Chorioptes equi* or the itchy leg mite and *Sarcoptes scabeie* which is known as the common mange mite which causes sarcoptic mange.

Mite infestation is called acariosis or acariasis. The good news about mites is that, unlike ticks, they don't transmit serious diseases to the host. Diagnosis is done by analysing a skin scraping from the affected equine.

Like lice, mites are a winter scourge and for the same reasons: animals are indoors, often in close proximity and their hair may be damper. A loss of condition and / or lowered immunity makes minis more susceptible to sarcoptic mange in particular. You can help to combat this by ensuring your donkey is well fed and kept dry so he or she is in good condition and has a strong immune system.

Although mite populations will be very significantly reduced in the warmer months, you need to try to protect your little equine and treat mange. You also can't only treat one member of the herd, even if it is the one most affected, as they can cross-infect each other.

Mange results in scabs and crusts on the skin. They can be quite thick and the mites stay buried in them where they lay eggs. When they hatch, the new generation of mites re-start the infestation and the mange symptoms become worse.

When it comes to treatment and prevention there are two problems. The first is that there are very few preparations that are designed to kill mites that are safe for use on equines. There are some including a dip, a powder and natural oil. Secondly, because the sarcoptic mite can be buried so deeply, any topical remedy must be vigorously and repeatedly applied so it penetrates the scabs and crusts deeply enough to reach the mites and eggs.

You need to be guided by your vet as to what to use and how to use it. It's also essential to clean out your pet's shelter or stall and treat it too before putting clean bedding back in.

There is also a type of mite that infests ears. As with other mites they won't cause serious health issues but the itching and discomfort can drive your mini a bit crazy. You will notice that your mini will rub its head and ears on objects and may shake its head a lot. If the rubbing is frequent and hard the ears may be rubbed raw, bruised or otherwise injured.

There are several products on the market that claim to deal with ear mites but they are not all safe for use on equines. Furthermore, some may be fine for horses but not donkeys. Some owners say that you can't, for example, use liquid solutions for minis but you can for horses.

Consult your vet about what product to use and how to administer it. If you have concerns, ask you vet if he or she is prepared to do it for you.

o) Stifle joint problems

The stifle joint is located fairly high up on the back legs near the hip. It's a complex joint that consists of three joint compartments:

the femoropatellar, medial femorotibial, and lateral femorotibial joints. All of them are stabilized by an equally complex network of ligaments which gives the stifle the ability to articulate through 150 degrees.

Causes and symptoms

It's not at all difficult to spot if your mini has a problem with this joint although it is a condition that develops very fast... and vanishes as quickly. It is far more common in minis that are three to twelve months old although it can occur for up to two years.

As the mini walks there is a popping action that makes it look as though a joint in the back leg has locked. The mini may even drag the back leg.

This is an intermittent and not an uncommon or a serious problem. It also looks far worse than it is and usually does not appear to cause pain or too much distress unless the leg drags or it happens very often.

The cause is straight-forward: a tight tendon within the stifle joint that is linked to changes in bone and soft tissue as young minis grow.

Treatment

Most minis outgrow stifle joint problems and don't require any treatment. In the rare case where this problem occurs daily or continues beyond two years, medication may be prescribed to help with inflammation and pain.

In the event that the tendon does not ease and becomes very tight, almost rigid, a simple surgical procedure may be necessary to correct this.

p) Bereavement

As previously stated, minis are highly social equines and they form very strong emotional bonds with the animal and human companions. The death of a companion is therefore a highly distressing and stressful time for your mini and it needs to be properly managed so your pet's health does not suffer.

➤ Let your mini stay with the body of its dead companion until it seems to lose interest and / or moves away. Like people, minis need to accept the loss. If they don't know their companion is gone forever, they will look for him or her and pine.

➤ Give the bereaved mini lots of extra cuddles and attention and spend more time with him or her if you can.

➤ Watch your mini's eating very carefully for several weeks. A grieving mini may stop eating, which will lead to weight and condition loss, a weakened immune system or even hyperlipaemia.

➤ Give your mini some extra treats such as warm water or some sweet nibbles like chopped apples or carrots. Just don't provide so many sugary treats that your mini puts on weight.

7) A Donkey First Aid Kit

While one can't prepare for every eventuality, it is a good idea to keep a first aid kit on hand so you can treat your little donkey immediately if the need arises. The basic kit, kept in a clearly marked, clean and air-tight container should include the following items:

- Disposable gloves (2 pairs)
- Gauze squares (various sizes)
- Gauze swabs (various sizes)
- First aid tape
- Rolls of gauze bandage
- Rolls of self-adhering bandage (sometimes called "vet wrap")
- Cotton wool (for foot pads or poultices *only*)
- Round-end scissors
- Tweezers
- Small torch
- Magnifying glass
- Various size syringes
- Rectal thermometer (ensure it is a suitable size for a mini)
- Lubricant
- Needle-nose pliers

- 20 gauge, 1" (2.5 centimetre) needles for adults if you give injections yourself
- 20 gauge, 1/2" (1.25 centimetres) needles for foals if you give injections yourself.

It's a good idea to also have a few medications in the kit. It is essential, though, to be guided by a breeder or your vet as to which ones will be safe for your pet. Basics could include:

- Poultice material
- Mild antiseptic / cleansing solution
- Mild antiseptic cream
- Epinephrine to counter anaphylactic shock.

Include details of the dates of vaccinations, deworming treatments and tetanus shots in case the vet needs this information or you are not there to provide it.

Collect all of the important emergency and other contact numbers such as the vet, farrier and equine dental technician. In an emergency one is not always thinking clearly so having the numbers you need to hand can save precious time. Have a card or list that includes your vet's number (including an after hours or emergency number), a local donkey sanctuary, the poison helpline and any other local resources that would be useful.

8) Pet medical aid

Having a sick Miniature Mediterranean Donkey is stressful and upsetting. It can also be very costly and these kinds of expenses are difficult to budget for.

If you give your mini the right diet, provide regular dental and hoof care and have vaccinations and boosters administered as and when required, your pet should stay pretty healthy. Of course, no animal is completely safe from illness and even the healthiest one can be injured.

Enter pet insurance. Depending on where you are you may be able to opt to take out one of several types of cover to help you with bills when your pint-sized equine needs medical care. Some insurers offer the choice of a plan that covers expenses in the event of an accident only. Others will pay costs for both accident and illness. The third option, one that usually gets added onto one of the others, is to cover standard procedures and costs such as vaccinations, deworming, dental treatments and routine farrier costs.

Like most insurance, these policies will have a deductible or excess that you will have to pay, but they can help greatly if your miniature donkey ever requires significant or ongoing treatment or vet care. The premium and affordability will also vary depending on the type of cover chosen and how many pets you place on the policy.

Your vet should be able to supply you with a brochure, pamphlet or information. You will have to weigh the cost of insurance against the possibility of being out of pocket at a later date.

Chapter 11: Miniature Donkey reproduction

Those fortunate enough to have miniature donkeys may be tempted to breed them, especially if they have an ungelded jack and several jennets. It's not as easy as it seems, though, and breeders have a responsibility to the species and anyone who buys one of their minis.

Early breeders had to focus to a large degree on increasing stock numbers. Now that the gene pools have grown significantly and are strong, the emphasis is on selective breeding so that the Miniature Mediterranean Donkeys produced are healthy, have the right temperaments and have the correct conformation including size. Good, responsible breeders are not breeding minis just for the money or to produce only one colour, for instance.

If you are ready for this responsibility and all the work that comes with it, you need to decide what your goals are before you invest in breeding stock.

1) Breeding Miniature Donkeys

People breed minis for two reasons: to produce lovable, loving and healthy pets or to produce donkeys that are all these things and make a valuable contribution to the gene pool. In essence the choice is between breeding for the pet market or for breeding programs. In either case, you need to breed the best minis you possibly can.

Your next phase of preparatory work is to learn all you can about animal husbandry. Try reliable online resources, books, set up an appointment with an equine vet, join interest groups and online forums where you can chat with other mini owners and – perhaps of particular value – find a mini breeder who is willing to be your mentor.

While there is work and serious responsibility involved, it is heartening to know that breeding and raising Miniature Donkeys is *much* easier than doing so with horses. For one thing you will probably not have to involve a vet because minis conceive and foal with ease.

New mothers are also much easier to work with as they are pretty relaxed and let their owner approach them and their baby. Your jennet will be happy to let you interact with her foal. As for the new arrival, even when it is very new, it will be friendly and it's not unknown for a foal to behave like a lap dog with its human.

Because there is such a demand for minis as pets, breeding them can generate a good income. However, this needs to be repeated: if you are only breeding minis for profit *don't*! You need to love these wonderful little equines and want to act in the individual and the species' best interests.

The financial aspects of breeding minis

If you own breeding stock with proven bloodlines that have produced high quality offspring and your minis are registered, you have a valuable asset. While minis won't generate the kind of money that horses do, they will provide a good source of income... and great emotional reward!

Of course like any other endeavour, breeding minis comes with expenses, both one-off and ongoing, and risks. Breeding minis does involve hard work, vigilance and commitment.

Furthermore, despite the best efforts of even experienced breeders not all foals born to breeding stock will be of the same quality. However, if the worst outcome is the production of a healthy and loving pet quality mini you are still doing well even if the profit margin is somewhat lower.

When to breed Miniature Donkeys

While some jacks may appear ready to breed when they are still very young and jennets may have their first heat cycle when they are still yearlings, don't breed them.

Donkeys don't become physically or emotionally fully mature before they are three years old. As a result you shouldn't breed with them before they are three or even four. There is plenty of time for your jennets to produce babies as they can continue to foal until they are in the twenties.

There are several reasons why waiting and being patient is essential. Firstly, jennets that have foals when they are too young can suffer irreversible physical damage that affects their muscular and skeletal systems. In addition, the foals themselves are more likely to be born with congenital defects. Very young jennets may also simply not be grown up enough emotionally to know how to mother a foal successfully.

Methods of breeding

Natural breeding

The simplest way to breed minis is natural breeding. Turn your jack out into pasture with a group of jennets and allow them to breed naturally. While this can be very successful and is unlikely to cause stress to your minis, there are potential disadvantages with the method:

- You may not know the breeding dates and therefore the foaling dates. This makes preparation for foaling more difficult.

- You may not be aware of whether your jack covered all the jennets in the herd or which ones were or were not bred with.

- Some jennets are not receptive and they may react very aggressively towards the jack. There is the risk of injury as a result.

- A jack may become aggressive towards a non-receptive jennet, which could also result in injuries.

These can all be overcome or controlled if you monitor and observe activities closely. There are other factors observation won't alleviate:

- If one of the minis in the herd is suffering from an infection it may be spread during breeding contact.

- Male foals may be perceived as a rival and a threat and the jack may try to kill them.

Hand breeding

The next option is called hand breeding. For this you will need a stall or a breeding chute in which the jennet will stand. The jack is led into the stall and controlled by you or a handler. While there are advantages to the technique there are draw-backs too.

The pros are:

✓ There are unlikely to be injuries as the process is controlled and closely monitored.

✓ If the jennet already has a foal it can be near her but not in the chute and therefore safe from the jack.

✓ The jack can conserve his energy because he doesn't have to pursue the jennets in a pasture setting.

✓ You will know exactly when your jack bred with which jennet and this will allow you to plan your foaling calendar accordingly and track foal's lineage.

The disadvantages are the need for a breeding chute or stall and it requires extra energy from you (and perhaps additional manpower too). Some jacks are slow to breed which can also make this method time consuming.

Artificial Insemination

Finally, you could elect to use artificial insemination (AI) as the method to breed minis. With AI, semen is collected from the jack. It is then used to artificially inseminate one or more jennets. The two choices here are to (a) use the services of a trained technician or (b) go on a course to learn how to perform AI and buy all the necessary equipment. Both of these options involve not inconsiderable costs.

On the up-side, AI reduces the chances of infection. As the jack and jennets don't actually come into contact there is no possibility of injury either. One can also impregnate a greater number of jennets using this method.

When can one rebreed?

A jennet will come into oestrus again about ten days after foaling. However, there are several reasons why she should not be bred again so soon.

Firstly, her reproductive system and tract will not yet be entirely settled and back to normal. Conceiving too soon may be detrimental to her and pose a risk to another foal. Secondly, the chances of conception are lower than usual so soon after foaling. Finally, she will still be very focused on her foal and protective of it and will therefore not react well to the presence of a jack.

It is recommended that you wait for two or three heats post foaling before breeding again. At this point the chances of conception are back to normal and the jennet is more relaxed. This means she will be more receptive to the jack and less concerned about her foal.

Given this waiting period before rebreeding and the gestation period for minis, you can count on each healthy jennet producing three foals every four years.

2) Reproduction

A discussion of reproduction focuses on the jennet, gestation, foaling and the care mother and baby require at each stage.

Oestrus

Jennets come into oestrus or heat every 21 to 28 days except during the winter months. This is the period during which ovulation takes place and when the female is sexually receptive and most likely to conceive.

The tell-tale indicators that a jennet is in this condition are that she will bray more than usual, may be a little irritable, will lay her ears flat, will urinate more frequently, may open and close her mouth in what is called a mouthing reflex and she may drool.

Gestation

There are several ways to diagnose a pregnancy in jennets and it's best to contact your vet in this regard. A pregnant jennet is usually relaxed and happy and will thrive best with her usual routine and companions.

While the average gestation period for Mediterranean Miniature Donkeys is 12 months, it can vary from 11 to 14 months.

Caring for your pregnant jennet

There is no need to introduce big changes in the like of a pregnant mini. Of course stress should be avoided and a quiet, relaxed life is ideal. If your jennet works (pulls a cart or gives rides, for example) that should be stopped for the final quarter of the pregnancy.

You need to ensure that your jennet is in optimal health during her pregnancy; continue with the usual hoof and dental care and de-worming program. However, it's a good idea to talk to your vet about the de-worming as it may not be needed and some products are not safe for expectant donkeys, especially in the final three months.

If your jennet is in good condition / at a good weight there is no need to alter her diet. Additional feed early in the pregnancy may lead to obesity, which poses a risk to both mother and baby. Additional food is needed, though, during the final three months when the unborn foal is growing very fast and for three months after foaling to promote and maintain lactation.

Foaling / the birth

Pre-birth

Although it is uncommon for there to be problems with foaling with minis, it's always wise to prepare and know how things will or should work. If you have any questions or concerns, talk to your mentor, the vet or staff at your local donkey sanctuary.

It's advisable to plan where the foal will be born. If it will be out of your jennet's usual stable or shelter for some reason you need to get her used to it gradually so as not to cause stress.

The site must be prepared for foaling: it needs to be cleaned and disinfected very thoroughly, be free of any objects that could injure the jennet or foal and clean, dry bedding must be put down. Don't use shavings as bedding because they may stick to the foal or get into its eyes. If the weather is cool then heating lamps might be a good idea.

Not all jennets behave the same way just before foaling. In fact the same jennet may not always behave the same way from one pregnancy to the next. But there are certain signs that are common to all jennets and indicate that foaling is not too far off or that the birth is imminent:

> The first change occurs about a month before the birth. The jennet's udder gradually increases in size.

> The teats undergo a change several days before foaling as the enlargement now extends all the way to the tip.

> At about 48 hours before foaling the teats develop a waxy cap.

> During the two to four days preceding foaling, some jennets have such engorged udders they may drip milk. *Don't* milk her.

> As the birth approaches, the pelvic ligaments begin to soften. As a result grooves form on either side of the jennet's spine near the tail head. These grooves are harder to spot if her coat is longer.

> In the week or two before foaling takes place, your jennet may become less social and prefer to be on her own.

> In the couple of weeks preceding the birth, the vulva gradually elongates and becomes very loose and soft.

> When the foal turns and gets ready to move into the birth canal, your jennet will appear restless and may even look

thinner. She may begin to walk up and down and may also lie down and then stand up again several times.

- ➢ With some jennets, foaling occurs immediately after the foal has turned. With other individuals it may take a few days before foaling begins.

- ➢ If the lips of the vulva are so swollen that they are flush with the hindquarters you can be confident that in a matter of hours the foal will arrive.

- ➢ Just before the foal is born you will notice that your jennet is holding her tail away from her body. It is often also slightly lifted and turned to one side.

- ➢ When birth is imminent the jennet may pass small amounts of urine and soft manure fairly frequently. This is as a result of the muscle contractions.

You need to be vigilant and watch your jennet for these signs. She may well decide that the middle of the night is a good time to give birth so you may need to make arrangements to have her monitored 24 hours a day.

You will know your jennet is in labour when the cervix is fully dilated. In addition, the water bag will protrude into the vagina and then rupture. This purpose of this fluid is to lubricate the birth canal and make it easier for the foal.

Your jennet knows what to do; she will begin to strain hard. It is usually not long until two tiny forefeet appear followed by the front legs. The foal's nose will be resting on its front legs. While this may look odd or even alarming this is the normal birthing position or presentation.

It's very important not to hurry or fluster the jennet. You must also never pull on the foal's feet thinking that will help or speed up the process. Even with a first foaling, a jennet will manage every aspect of the birth on her own. Most mini births only take between 15 and 30 minutes.

Even though complications are very rare they can happen. If after twenty minutes of hard straining there is still no sign of the foal's feet, or only one foot appears or the forelegs are out but not the nose, you must call the vet. Malpresentation of this kind poses a great threat to both the foal and the jennet and it's not something a layperson can deal with. Your jennet and her unborn foal need help from a professional or an expert or they may suffer injury or one or both may not survive.

As the foal's neck appears, the baby may begin to move its head. This movement will probably break the membrane that covers the foal. If it doesn't, you need to carefully tear it open and gently wipe the foal's nose to clear the mucous from its nostrils. This will help it to breathe.

What you mustn't do is cut the navel or umbilical cord when the foal has emerged completely. After the birth the jennet will get to her feet. This movement breaks the cord. Once it has broken, you can dip the end of the cord into a 5% iodine solution. This protects against possible infection.

Post-birth

With a normal birth the jennet will then begin to lick her foal. This performs several very important functions: it helps to build the bond between the mother and her baby, it stimulates the foal's circulation and it dries the foal and prevents it becoming chilled.

Within half an hour of giving birth the jennet will manage to expel the afterbirth or placenta. If after six hours this has still not occurred, you need to call the vet because a retained placenta can result in an infection or inflammation.

Foals weigh on average approximately 20 pounds or a mere 9 kilograms when they are born. They also only stand at between 18 and 24 inches or 45 and 60 centimetres.

You need to stay to make sure that, once dry, the foal also stands and begins to nurse or feed. These first feeds are essential to the foal's health as the first milk, called colostrum, is very rich in antibodies.

If the jennet doesn't want to let her foal nurse – and this may happen with first-time mothers – you will need to intervene. You will have to hold or even tie your jennet and help the foal to nurse.

Fortunately you will probably only have to do this once or twice and then the jennet's instincts will kick in.

The other milestone you need to check on is that the foal has passed its first dropping, which is called the meconium. This usually takes place when the foal struggles to its feet for the first time and consists of hard pellets.

If this has not been passed during the first 24 hours of life and if the foal shows clear signs of trying to defecate such as straining and lifting its tail, you must call in a vet. The vet will either give the foal a dose of mineral oil that acts as a laxative or will administer an enema.

It is not uncommon for foals to suffer from diarrhoea, also known as scours, when they are seven or ten days old. This coincides with the first time since foaling the jennet comes into heat. This first oestrus after birth is called "foal heat". The foal should be back to normal after a few days. However, if the diarrhoea continues and / or the foal just doesn't seem well you need to consult a vet. Diarrhoea in any very young animal is potentially dangerous and should not be ignored.

While adult minis are pretty hardy creatures, the same can't be said for very young foals. The fact that these babies have fluffy coats also gives the false impression that they are well insulated. Very young minis are in fact not hardy and become chilled easily. As a result they must be kept warm and sheltered. This is particularly important for the first two weeks following birth.

Foals that get too cold or get wet must be dried off and warmed immediately as these babies are highly susceptible to respiratory infections such as pneumonia and bronchitis. Serious infections like these may be fatal for very young miniatures.

Two weeks or a month after birth, the foal will begin to eat small amounts of their mother's feed. However, their bodies have not adapted enough at this stage to be able to gain nutrition from this feed. But this is a signal to you to start feeding a foal commercial feed. The baby should be fed separately in a pen next to the jennet but where the mother can't get in and eat the foal's ration.

A mini foal can be weaned anywhere from six to 12 months. Don't wean a baby when it is younger than three months unless you do so at a vet's recommendation for the sake of the foal or the jennet. Premature weaning will have long-term effects on the health and behaviour of a donkey. Foals weaned too young will require a considerable amount of extra care and attention to try to remedy the damage done.

On the other end of the scale, a foal that is weaned too late will be very traumatised by being taken from his mother, as their bond will be especially strong. The absolute oldest age for weaning a mini foal is considered to be nine months. The jennet's milk is less nutritious by this stage which is a further reason why weaning must be done earlier.

Chapter 12: Costs & where to buy a donkey

1) Costs

The price of Miniature Mediterranean Donkeys is highly variable and affected by a number of factors. These include height (the smaller the donkey is the more it will cost), gender (jennets generally cost more than jacks), colour, conformation and registration.

The price of Miniature Mediterranean Donkeys

At time of writing, you will pay in the region of $500 - $800 or £410 - £655 for a young gelding that is a pet quality. A show gelding will cost on average $2500 or £2050. Even minis with a popular or less common coat colour could be as much as $5000 or £4100.

Breeding stock is far more expensive and a jack from a proven bloodline will sell for $2000 to $6000 or £1640 - £4920. Some jennets with strong bloodlines have sold for a staggering $10000 or £8200!

Keep in mind that you don't have to start with breed quality stock. With a pet make sure the individual is healthy, a good size and friendly. If it is also a colour you like that's a bonus. When or if you are ready to move into breeding minis, though, you can't really go wrong if you check conformation and genetics before investing in a mini.

Some breeders believe that if you are going to buy a mini with the intention of breeding minis you should buy the best you can afford. After all, it costs the same to feed and care for mini regardless of bloodline or quality. If your stock produces high quality foals you will get a far greater return on your investment.

As you grow your business you can invest in better and better bloodlines, which will benefit the species as a whole. You will reach a point where your minis pay for themselves. Just keep in mind that while you will generate some income, nobody got rich from breeding minis and it's certainly not a get-rich-quick scheme.

Other one-off costs

If you already have a suitable shelter and a fenced off pasture area of the right size, your initial capital outlay will be fairly modest. If you need to invest in these types of structures, getting ready to own minis won't be cheap.

For example, ten treated wood fence posts will cost in the region of £23 or $28 and 400 meters or 1312 feet of battery powered electric fencing sells for about £250 or $305.

While this is not an exhaustive list, you will need to invest in the following items:

- Blanket: £16 - 74 / $20 - 90
- Broom: £6 - 8 / $7.50 - 10
- Buckets: (2): £8 - 16 / $10 - 20
- Fork: £12 - 16 / $15 - 19
- Grooming kit: £20 - 50 / $24 - 61
- Poop-scoop: £15 - 24 / $18 - 29
- Rake: £11 - 23 / $12 - 16
- Rope halter: £15 - 20 / $18 - 25
- Shovel: £10 - 25 / $12 - 30
- Wheelbarrow: £41 - 164 / $50 - 200.

Some of these items like blankets and halters will need to be replaced as they become worn. Other items are much harder wearing and will not need replacing for quite some time.

Ongoing expenses

Several owners and breeders, at time of writing, believe that the annual cost per mini is $400 - $640 or £330 - £525. This is assuming that the donkey is healthy and that you don't need to provide extra feed, which can happen. You may need, for instance, to buy in feed in summer if a drought has caused poor grazing conditions.

You will also have to budget for annual vet and farrier expenses for vaccinations, boosters and dental check-ups. At time of writing average price ranges were:

- Vet call-out and examination fee: £20 – 80 / $25 - 98
- Dental check-up: £20 – 50 / $25 - 61 *
- Farrier (check and trim): £12 – 30 / $15 - 37 *
- Annual flu and tetanus shot: £50 / $61
- Tetanus booster: £30 – 45 / $37 - 55
- Faecal egg count test: £35 / $43 *
- Annual deworming (based on 3 treatments): £16 – 40 / $19.50 – 49.

The expenses marked with an asterisk are for a single check-up, faecal egg count test or, in the case of the farrier, one hoof trim. However, there will be more than one of each per annum per mini. For example, a farrier should see your pet roughly every two months and regular dental checks are essential too.

If your mini develops a serious or a chronic medical condition or sustains an injury, you will be faced with far higher expenses than those outlined above. With chronic conditions these costs will be ongoing and could be not just hundreds but thousands of Dollars or Pounds. Health insurance for your mini is certainly worth investigating and considering seriously.

In terms of feed, prices vary greatly depending on area, season and weather conditions. It is estimated that each mini requires one bale of hay a week during the months that pasture grazing is either unavailable or must be supplemented because it is of poor quality.

If hay costs £4 to £7 or $5 to $8.50 per bale and you buy bales for half the year, the annual cost will be £104 to £182 or $127 to $222 per mini. Of course price is affected by bale size and type, the composition of the hay and where it comes from. These prices are based on small bales that have been locally sourced.

Bedding material also needs to be factored in as an ongoing cost. If you use straw for both feeding and bedding you should probably budget for 100 bales per annum per mini. Straw bale costs also vary depending on a number of factors but a small bale costs in the region of £3.50 or $4.30.

2) Where you can buy a mini

You can buy Miniature Donkeys from breeders (both registered and not), from donkey sanctuaries, at auctions and online. If you have joined an online forum or group you could ask the other members for suggestions or recommendations. Mini owners will be quick to offer each other suggestions and warnings about what to do or avoid!

Breeders are probably the best bet, especially if you want to invest in breeding stock. In addition, if you want a jack or a jennet with a proven bloodline you will need a registered breeder.

Donkey sanctuaries are a wonderful place to buy or adopt pets but make sure you are buying a mini that is healthy. It's fine to buy a mini that's not all that young anymore as long as it is healthy. Most sanctuaries are run by caring professionals who will be honest about the minis in their care.

However, there's no harm in asking someone with experience to go with you if you aren't sure what to look for. Those who adopt sanctuary minis sometimes don't mind taking on a donkey with some issues. That's a personal decision.

Equine auctions can be very good places to buy minis. You should have an opportunity to look at the minis on sale before the auction itself and to get information about them. Again, ask someone with knowledge of minis (and maybe experience at auctions) to go with you.

Don't ever buy a miniature donkey sight unseen! If you see a mini advertised online or elsewhere you must meet it and have a chance to arrange a vet examination if you want to do so.

3) Finding and selecting a breeder

There are a number of farms and stables that advertise themselves and their Miniature Mediterranean Donkeys but how do you know if it is a breeder that is entirely trustworthy? One option is that you can visit the websites of donkey associations to see if the breeder is listed or registered with them. The second option is to ask the breeder for proof of registration.

Of course if you are looking for a pet mini rather than breeding stock you may not really be concerned about having the 'right' paperwork to show that a breeder is registered or that the minis they produce are. Your concerns will probably be that the mini you are interested in is healthy and the right age.

If a breeder won't or can't provide medical records such as proof of vaccinations, worry. If a breeder won't allow you to have a vet examine a mini, go somewhere else.

In addition, if you are specifically buying breeding stock from a registered or professional breeder you should ask for a guarantee of fertility for the jack or jennet you are buying. If you later discover that the mini is not able to breed or conceive you have the right to go back to the breeder to recover all or part of your money, depending on the terms of the guarantee.

Some breeders will offer more general health guarantees that offer protection against congenital health problems or severe behavioural problems. In these situations, the breeder may agree to take the mini back. A word of caution: don't allow a breeder to sell a 'problem' mini on your behalf. The next owner will want compensation from you if they were not told of the issues.

Don't be blinded by how sweet and cute minis are. Don't allow a breeder to rush you or get pushy. Take your time. Ask someone with more knowledge to help you decide if you are still inexperienced. If properly cared for, a mini will be part of your life for several decades. Make sure you are right for each other.

Chapter 13: Conclusion

A Miniature Mediterranean Donkey makes a wonderful pet and companion. While they will love and entertain you and be loyal and affectionate companions for decades, they need a great deal from you in return.

As a loving and responsible mini owner you will have to make sure that your donkey has all that it requires in order to be healthy and happy. Minis have physical, emotional, intellectual and social needs that must be met.

Their physical requirements include a good, healthy diet that is high in fibre and very low in protein, sugar and grains; regular vet, dental and farrier check-ups and care; preventative care in the form of vaccinations and deworming; restricted access to safe pasture and 24 hour access to clean, dry shelter and water.

These little equines need daily handling, affectionate interaction with their owners and play-time. You need to provide objects they can safely play and interact with that provide fun and the mental stimulation these intelligent equines must have in order to be happy. Training also affords them important interaction and stimulation.

Last but not least, while your mini will bond with you and love you they should still ideally have the company of another mini. A mini can certainly have a happy and fulfilling life without a same-species friend and will form other bonds... but it's just not the same.

1) Safety tips

You are your mini's protector and part of your job is to protect it from harm. While nobody can guard against every threat and eventuality there are certain things you can do:

o   Ensure that all fences are intact and strong so predators, including domestic dogs, can't attack your mini.

o Check the pasture and boundary regularly for toxic plants. If any are found remove them and dispose of them safely.

o Don't leave a halter on your donkey when it is unattended in case it gets snagged on something and leads to injury or worse.

2) Care schedule

Looking after an equine can be daunting if you look at a list of what must be done. What makes it much easier and much less scary is to break tasks down.

Daily tasks

- Feed your mini
- Clean or muck out your mini's shelter
- Remove droppings from the pasture
- Observe your mini for any changes in behaviour or demeanour
- Clean out water containers and refill them with clean water
- Pick out your minis feet if the ground is wet and damp
- Spend some cuddle and bonding time
- Apply insect repellent if necessary.

Weekly tasks

- Check fences and fence posts to ensure they are still sound
- Groom your mini
- Patrol for toxic plants and remove and safely dispose of any you find
- Clean water containers in the pasture area and refill them
- Clean and disinfect your mini's shelter.

Monthly tasks

- Arrange a visit from the farrier (every *two* months)
- Measure your mini's girth and weight.

Annual and bi-annual tasks

- Schedule a check-up with an equine dental technician *twice* yearly
- Schedule an appointment with the vet for a check-up, annual vaccinations
- Arrange a faecal egg count test *twice* yearly and any de-worming that becomes necessary
- Perform maintenance work on fencing, flooring and the shelter.

What needs to be done in spring

- Begin to gradually introduce pasture grazing
- Check for any toxic plants
- Launch fly and other insect repellent programs
- Clean or muck out your mini's shelter

What needs to be done in summer

- Increase grooming to help remove your mini's winter coat
- Fence off fruit trees that are accessible
- Monitor girth and weight and control grazing accordingly
- Continue with insect control measures

What needs to be done in autumn

- Replace worn or old rugs or blankets
- Lay in feed and bedding supplies for autumn and winter use
- Place bark chips on any areas that are likely to get muddy and damp such as gateways
- Fence off oak trees
- Treat wooden fencing and buildings to protect against rain and snow

What needs to be done in winter

- Make sure that your mini has hard, dry surfaces to stand on
- Keep your mini dry to prevent it becoming chilled

- Provide tepid or warm water and monitor water intake
- Remove rugs for some time each day to prevent moisture build-up under them.

2) Do's... in no particular order

✓ Learn about Miniature Mediterranean Donkeys in particular and donkeys generally. Buy books, watch videos, talk to experts or attend a course at a donkey sanctuary.

✓ Take the time to bond with your mini and to get to know it really well in terms of both personality and behaviour.

✓ Learn how to take your mini's temperature (not fun for either of you but it could save your mini's life).

✓ Be aware of any changes in your pet's eating or drinking patterns, its behaviour or frequency or consistency of its faeces as these are excellent indicators of health or illness. Remember minis are stoic so you need to spot problems.

✓ Make sure that your mini's shelter is dry, clean and draft-, pest- and vermin-free.

✓ Train your donkey and start doing so almost immediately.

✓ Give your mini toys.

✓ Ensure your mini receives all the necessary vaccines, boosters and de-worming at the right times.

✓ Make sure your donkey has regular check-ups with the vet, dental technician and farrier.

✓ If you don't want to breed minis, have your jack gelded.

✓ Take steps to keep ticks, flies, midges, mites and lice away.

✓ Feed your mini the right diet and always supply fresh, clean water.

✓ Keep an equine First Aid Kit and contact list handy.

✓ If your mini must be hospitalised, its companion animal must go with it to reduce stress as it can lead to complications or other conditions.

3) Don'ts... in no particular order

- Don't restrict food intake as extreme dieting can put minis at risk of developing hyperlipaemia.

- Neglect vaccinations and vet, dental and farrier check-ups.

- Ignore signs of changes in behaviour and demeanour.

- Separate your mini from its companion.

- Deworm your mini more often than is necessary.

- Feed your mini sugary treats

4) And in closing...

This guide's primary purpose is to make sure that you have the information that you need to decide, first and foremost, if this is *really* the right pet for you, for your spouse, for your child or for your lifestyle.

If the answer is a confident and honest "Yes", this pet owner's guide will also give you the details that will help you to keep your Miniature Donkey healthy and happy.

If you are one of those individuals who commits to owning and caring for one of these amazing little equines you will be rewarded by having a pet that is sweet natured, loving, smart, full of beans and has loads of personality!

Enjoy your Miniature Mediterranean Donkey and teach others about them!

Published by IMB Publishing 2016

Made in the USA
Monee, IL
27 November 2020